The Small Church IS Different!

The Small Church IS Different!

Lyle E. Schaller

ABINGDON PRESS
Nashville

THE SMALL CHURCH IS DIFFERENT!

Library of Congress Cataloging in Publication Data

SCHALLER, LYLE E.
  The small church is different!
  1. Small churches. I. Title.
  BV637.8.S3   254'.2   82-1830   AACR2

ISBN 0-687-38717-5

MANUFACTURED BY THE PARTHENON PRESS AT
NASHVILLE, TENNESSEE, UNITED STATES OF AMERICA

CONTENTS

*To our friends and teachers
at Briggsville, Moundville, and Endeavor
who patiently and lovingly taught us
so much about the small church*

PREFACE

The normal size for a Protestant congregation on the North American continent is one that has fewer than forty people at worship on the typical Sunday morning.

That sentence belongs in the same category of descriptive statements as these. Water runs downhill. After his thirty-fifth birthday, the average American male gains a pound in weight every year. The buying power of the dollar in 1983 was approximately one third what it was in 1965. As the number of people belonging to an organization goes up, the percentage of members attending a regular meeting tends to go down. The larger the number of people attending a meeting or a conference, the smaller the proportion who will feel free to speak during the formal session. The eight-year-old is convinced that each year is seven hundred days in length, the thirty-year-old believes a year has close to four hundred days, the fifty-year-old thinks it is closer to three hundred, and the sixty-five-year-old person knows it is less than two hundred.

A persuasive argument can be made that each of the above statements describes one slice of reality. That does not mean that every one of these statements should be evaluated as good. That does not mean we are helpless victims of these descriptive statements. Every year, people spend billions of dollars to make water run uphill. Every year thousands of males who believe in open-casket funerals jog, play tennis or handball, diet, and take other steps to offset the forces of nature and gravity, so that some day in the future the mourners will be able to look in the casket and exclaim, "Doesn't he look good!" Every year,

9

hundreds of proposals are developed to offset the impact of inflation. Every year, leaders plead with the members of their organization to attend more frequently. Every year, organizers of conferences invent new ways of giving every attender a chance to be an active participant. Every year, manufacturers turn out calendars based on the assumption that three out of four years contain exactly 365 days.

What does all of that have to do with the small membership church? The answer to that question can be summarized by three words: perspective, policies, and priorities.

The first is the matter of perspective. The person who turns the faucet in the second floor bathroom rarely marvels that water flows freely out of that faucet. Today, people accept as a fact of life that water can be made to run uphill. A parallel can be found in the fact that one seventh of all Protestant congregations in the United States and Canada include more than one-half of all church members, and also provide a substantial majority of our denominational leaders. Their perspective causes most of them to underestimate the very large number of small-membership congregations. Today, many church leaders appear to assume that the very large congregation is the normative institutional expression of the Christian congregation.

From this writer's perspective, the facts suggest that the natural size of the worshiping congregation is that of the small church. This thesis can be supported by a variety of data. At the end of 1980, one half of the 8,832 congregations in the United Presbyterian Church reported a communicant membership of 178 or less. Three quarters of the congregations in the Christian Church (Disciples of Christ) have fewer than 255 participating members. Two thirds of all United Methodist congregations in the United States average less than one hundred at the principal weekly worship service. Fifty-five percent of all congregations in the Lutheran Church in America have fewer than two hundred confirmed members. Nearly three fourths of the congregations in the Presbyterian Church in the U.S. include fewer than 250 members. One half of all Southern Baptist churches report an average attendance of less than seventy in Sunday School, and two thirds report an average of less than 102. Two thirds of all United Church of Christ congregations include fewer than 300 members. One half of the congregations in the Baptist General Conference average less than 105 at worship on Sunday morning. In Canada, the proportion of small congregations is higher in most denominations than it is for their counterparts in the United States.

The small church is the normative institutional expression of the worshiping congregation among the Protestant denominations on the North American continent. One fourth of all Protestant congregations on this continent have fewer than thirty-five people in attendance at the principal weekly worship service, and one half average less than seventy-five.

Despite the fact that most Protestant congregations can be classified as "small churches," the dominant perspective of most church leaders is that of the large church. One obvious reason for that is that a majority of the members and most of the denominational leaders are in large congregations. Most church members and leaders have become accustomed to the style of congregational life, the division of responsibilities between the laity and the clergy, the schedule, and the program of the large church. That is what they know first-hand. They naturally see that as "the way the world is." They also have become accustomed to a water pipe that enters the building below ground level and enables that second-floor faucet to produce a supply of water. That does not mean, however, that water naturally runs uphill.

In a similar manner, the large congregation runs against

the laws of nature—even in southern California and Texas. The continued existence of that large congregation requires the sustained efforts of many people to keep that water running uphill. When that sustained effort begins to diminish, these large churches tend to decline in size. One example of this is the decrease in the number of United Methodist congregations with a thousand or more members—from 2106 in 1970, to 1485 in 1979. A similar pattern can be seen in the United Presbyterian Church, as the number of large churches dropped from 598 in 1970, to 420 in 1978. Unless people keep pumping, the water that was running uphill begins to run downhill.

By contrast, most small congregations tend to stay on the same plateau in size, year after year and decade after decade, just as water tends to find its own level. Or, to carry the parallel one step further, it is not uncommon to see large congregations shrink in size, but it is unusual for the long-established congregation averaging thirty, forty, or fifty at worship to double or triple in size.

This book is written from a perspective that assumes the small-membership church is consistent with the natural order of creation. Thus it differs substantially from the large-membership church, in which a great deal of effort must be expended to maintain a big operation. The large church is not an enlarged version of the small congregation, and the small-membership church is not a miniature replica of the big church.

To switch analogies, the congregation averaging less than 35 or 40 at worship can be represented by an acorn squash, the church averaging 125 at worship can be depicted by a pumpkin, the congregation averaging 200 at worship might be portrayed by a horse, and the huge church averaging 500 or 600 or more at worship can be symbolized by a fifteen-room house. They are not simply different size specimens from the same genus or species. They are almost as different from one another as a village is unlike a large central city. It is impossible to produce a pumpkin by combining three acorn squashes. The person who is very competent in raising pumpkins may not be an expert at caring for horses. The fifteen-room house requires both maintenance and a different kind of care than the garden in which one raises squash and pumpkins. A different perspective and a different set of criteria should be used in grading squash or pumpkins than would be used in judging a horse or appraising a large house.

In summary, people involved in small-membership churches will find it helpful to look at the world from a different perspective from what is appropriate for understanding the large congregation.

The first chapter of this volume represents an effort to identify and lift up some of the unique characteristics of the small-membership church. After these differences have been identified, it is easier to recognize and respond to the implications of these differences.

There is always the risk of oversimplifying life whenever any one perspective is used to examine reality. For example, the degree of *heterogeneity* in a congregation is, in fact, a function of size; but it is also a function of the community context, the length of the time the congregation has been in existence, and the tenure of the current pastor. In general, the small church tends to have a higher degree of homogeneity within the membership than is found in large congregations, but there are hundreds of exceptions to that statement. These include that very large, but remarkably homogeneous, German Baptist congregation in South Dakota, that small and very heterogeneous biracial church in Georgia, that large and homogeneous church in Jackson, Mississippi, and that very large, thirty-year-old congregation in California still served by the founding pastor.

One result is that there may be little change in the

perspective of the person who goes to the relatively new, very large, and highly homogeneous congregation after having spent several years in a much smaller homogeneous congregation. This experience may produce the statement, "I don't think size makes that much difference."

That statement represents the perspective of the person who sees homogeneity and heterogeneity as more influential than size in understanding the dynamics of congregational life.

The second word that is essential in understanding the distinctive character and role of the small-membership church is *policies*. This includes both the official policies and the informal operational policies. For example, in many denominations there is a broad policy that encourages long pastorates in large-membership churches. The unofficial, or informal, policy begins to question the competence, the ambition, or the responsiveness of the minister who has been serving the same small-membership church for ten consecutive years.

Far more significant, however, is the basic denominational policy that recommends the same system of church government, the same standards for church finances, the same approach to Christian education, and the same questions for congregational reporting, regardless of the size of the church involved. The inventor who manufactures his new invention in the family garage has a different type of business than General Motors—and the Internal Revenue Service has radically different policies for the reporting system required of each one.

The second, third, and fourth chapters of this volume discuss a half-dozen areas of congregational life in which size is a very significant factor in planning, policy formulation, and goal setting for congregations of different sizes. Additional policy questions regarding the small-membership church are raised in the fifth chapter.

The third word that helps to explain the distinctive character of the small-membership church is *priorities*. The priorities of the small church are different from those encountered in large Protestant congregations. A simple example is corporate worship. The average attendance at worship in the small-membership church usually is a figure equal to between 70 and 120 percent of the reported membership. It is rare to find a two-thousand-member congregation in which the average attendance at worship exceeds 50 percent of the membership.

The small congregation places a higher priority on relationships, on the importance of everyone's being able to call all other members by name, on the rights and privileges of each individual, and on making sure all the bills are paid. The large church places a higher priority on the functional aspects of ministry, on a carefully administered organizational structure, on the smooth operation of that large institution, and on a systematic approach to fund-raising and stewardship.

Some readers may conclude that this book is an uncritical apologetic for the small-membership church. Others may conclude that the treatment is harsh and unsympathetic. Both will be able to find sentences to support their positions. The central purpose has not been to be either defensive or critical, but rather to insist that the unique characteristics of the small-membership church mean that it would be unwise, and often counterproductive, to attempt to force large-church ideas, rules, programs, procedures, and models on these smaller congregations. The small church is different! Recognize and affirm those differences.

Finally, in closing, it may be acceptable to offer one defensive observation. To paraphrase Abraham Lincoln, God must love the small church. He made so many of them.

Chapter I

IT IS DIFFERENT!

I'm worried," declared Karl Spencer, as he stopped raking leaves one Saturday afternoon in October and walked across the yard to chat with his neighbor, Harold Yoder. After taking early retirement following thirty-five years of employment with a steel company, Karl and Irene Spencer had moved to this small Iowa town to be near one of their children. Now, two years later, they were among the most active members of the 97-member congregation in which Harold Yoder was clearly the leading layman.

"The year's more than three-quarters gone, and we've paid less than a third of what we're expected to pay for missions and denominational obligations. Now we get the news that we've got to spend $2500 for a new heating system. Where are we going to get the money? I talked with the treasurer about it down at the post office this morning, and she told me she only has enough money in the bank to pay the current bills," continued Karl, with a worried expression on his face.

"Don't worry, Karl," assured Harold. "We'll make it; we always have in the past, and we'll make it this year."

"You sure sound pretty confident," replied Karl, "but I'm not. We've never been in a church that didn't pay its fair share of denominational apportionments, and I'm not comfortable with the possibility that we may end up paying for that new furnace out of what we should be giving for missions."

"We'll make it," repeated Harold Yoder with a completely confident tone of voice. "Our people will respond to the need. They always have in the past, and they will again this year. Don't worry about it, Karl."

"Well, maybe so, but I sure would be more comfortable if we had our missions pledge paid," responded Karl. "I think what we ought to do is to include $500, or maybe even a thousand, in the budget each year as reserves for a trustees' fund so we wouldn't get caught with these big bills unexpectedly."

"Sounds like a good idea," agreed Harold, "but I don't think our people would buy it. Here, we're used to being challenged to rise to the occasion, and somehow or another we always make it."

Harold is right. One of the distinctive characteristics of thousands of small-membership churches is that they usually manage their finances in a more informal and less systematic way than that followed in large congregations.

"When they understand the need, our people will respond," is the assurance given by thousands of lay persons every year to recently arrived and worried ministers who envision financial calamity only a few months away.

Karl Spencer, who had spent nearly four decades of his life in large urban churches before moving to this small Iowa community, also was vulnerable to this irrelevant concern. He had been trained to be comfortable with a careful and systematic long-range approach to church finances. He needed more than two years to learn to be comfortable with the more informal approach used by the typical small congregation. One reason why small-membership congregations are so tough, (in contrast to the institutional fragility of the typical huge congregation) is that the members do rally around and respond to a clear and visible need. While the per-member giving level of the typical small-membership church is lower than in the typical large congregation,[1] the dependability of the people in responding in a time of need is one of the distinctive characteristics of the small congregation.

It Is Different!

Another perspective on the differences between small-membership churches and larger congregations can be illustrated by listening in on two brief conversations.

"I guess the flu season has finally ended," remarked Edna Doyle as she greeted her friend, Marge Harmon, following the close of the Sunday morning worship service at Bethel Church. This ninety-year-old congregation met in a white frame building out in the open country, and that Sunday morning there had been 32 people in attendance. "Yes," replied Marge, "everyone was here today. It's been at least six or seven weeks since we had everybody here on the same Sunday."

"I can remember when Reverend Harrison was here; we used to fill this place Sunday after Sunday," reminisced Harold Murphy, a 63-year-old usher at the 900-member Hillside Church. "Today we had only half a crowd, and at least a dozen pews were completely empty. We sure aren't attracting the crowds we had ten years ago."

These two conversations illustrate three interesting differences among congregations. First, one of the basic differences between large churches and small congregations is how the members "take attendance." In the typical small congregation the members note who is absent and who is present. By contrast, in many larger churches it is impossible for any one person to keep track of every other member. Therefore the typical member is more likely to note the overall size of the crowd and to be more conscious of the vacant pews. In small churches the members count faces. In large churches they count the furniture.

Second, these two conversations illustrate the fact that, in the small congregations, the primary focus tends to be on the health of each individual, while in the large churches the primary focus tends to be on the congregation as a whole and on its institutional health. In small churches people tend to emphasize their relationships with one another. By contrast, in large congregations the members tend to focus their attention on the institution.

Third, the congregation of 250 people gathering to worship in a facility designed to seat 600 usually will experience a psychological defeat when that room is more than half-empty. By contrast, the congregation of thirty-five "regulars" can meet year after year in a building designed to seat ninety persons and be completely oblivious to those empty pews, as long as every one of the regulars is present or accounted for. Some factors that are very important in one size congregation are irrelevant in other size churches.

"Why don't we ask Pete Hanson to be a trustee next year?" suggested one member of the nominating committee as they met to prepare a slate of officers for the coming year for the 197-member Trinity Church.

"Are you kidding?" responded another member of the committee. "I doubt if Pete has been in church a total of ten Sundays during the past three years. Besides that, I don't think he has been able to hold a job for more than six months at a time. Why in the world do you suggest he should become a trustee?"

"Well, his father and grandfather both were trustees here for many, many years, and his father-in-law was our treasurer for nearly thirty years before he died," came the response from the person who had suggested Pete's name. "I think Pete's old enough now that he'll begin to settle down. Maybe if we make him a trustee, he'll become more active."

"I think it's worth considering," agreed the third member of the nominating committee. "Pete's married now, his wife's parents were very active here when they were alive, Pete and Helen are expecting a baby in a few months, and I believe electing Pete to be a trustee might help him settle down and accept responsibilities."

It Is Different!

This conversation illustrates two more distinctive characteristics of many small-membership churches. First, in long-established small congregations, bloodlines can be very influential in selecting officers. People who come from a long line of very active and committed church members are more likely to be chosen at a relatively young age for important leadership positions than members who do not have the benefit of good bloodlines. In some congregations it is even possible to acquire a respected pedigree through the right marriage, although that usually is easier for men to accomplish than it is for women.

Second, thousands of small-membership congregations act on the premise that the office can mold the person. Every year, all across this continent, members who have been relatively inactive and irresponsible in fulfilling their vows of membership are asked to accept responsible leadership positions in small-membership congregations. One reason, obviously, is the shortage of personnel and the desire "to spread the load around a little more." Another reason, however, is the expectation, often based on historical precedent, that a church leadership role has the power to change behavior patterns.

By contrast, in most large congregations, a member has to "earn" the privilege of being nominated as a leader by (a) serving as a worker for several years, (b) bringing impressive credentials as a lay leader when transferring in from another congregation, or (c) holding an influential secular position that causes other church members to credit the holder of that position (such as banker, superintendent of schools, proprietor of a small business, or large-scale farmer) with unusual leadership capabilities.

It was her first funeral service and the Reverend Susan Peters was more than slightly nervous. Three weeks earlier she had arrived to begin her first regular pastorate. The

164-member church was one of four congregations with a meeting house in this New England community of 700 residents. Two days earlier, a man whom she had never met, but who was a member of a "fringe family" of this one-hundred-forty-three-year-old congregation, had died very suddenly. The funeral director had called her, and she had hurried over to the funeral home where she had met this man's wife, also for the first time. The widow asked Susan if she would conduct the funeral service. By two o'clock on this rainy Thursday afternoon, Susan was fully prepared to conduct her first funeral service. By ten minutes to two, all but the front pews in the small, white frame building had been filled, and the ushers were bringing in chairs. When Susan stepped into the chancel to begin the service, she saw people sitting on the steps leading to the two classrooms on the second floor, and the narthex was filled with people standing.

Later that afternoon, Susan asked one of the leaders of the congregation, "Why was there such a big crowd today? I never dreamed there would be this many people to turn out for a funeral on a Thursday afternoon. What does this mean?"

"Death is important here, Reverend," was the response. "In this town, people turn out for a funeral, even if it means taking time off from work."

This was a new experience for Susan Peters. She had been born and reared in Philadelphia and had grown up in a much larger congregation. During her intern year as a seminarian, she had served as a staff member in an 1800-member congregation. She had assisted in conducting a half-dozen funeral services in that congregation, but only once had the crowd exceeded one hundred and fifty people.

The Reverend Susan Peters soon learned that the death of a member in the small-membership church is often a bigger event than is the death of a member in the large church, especially if that small congregation is located in a small community.

In the small church, the death of a member is more than simply one of the 5,400 deaths recorded on an average day in the United States, or one of the 500 deaths recorded on an average day in Canada. It often means the loss of a friend, a conspicuously empty pew the following Sunday, and may also mean the death of a relative. In the larger congregation, death usually is much more impersonal and the loss is not as obvious, except to a few. In the small congregation, one death may mean the loss of five percent of the adult leadership. In the large church, the death of a member may be only a decrease of one-tenth of one percent in the membership.

"I think we ought to set aside one day some time this fall and take a look at our program plans for the next two or three years," suggested the Reverend Steve Wagner, the twenty-nine-year-old minister of the 168-year-old Bethany Church. Steve had arrived fifteen months earlier after three years as the associate minister of a larger congregation. He had gone directly to that congregation following graduation from seminary.

"That's a good idea," agreed Marilyn Barrett, a long-time leader at Bethany. Marilyn was very active in a number of community groups and organizations and was remarkably articulate. While twenty years older than Steve, Marilyn saw the new minister as the best thing that had happened to this 193-member congregation in years.

After several minutes of discussion, Marilyn moved that a Saturday in October be set aside as a planning day. The motion was seconded and carried. During the next several months, Steve, Marilyn, and two other members met regularly to develop the schedule for this planning retreat.

When the appointed Saturday rolled around, only six

people showed up, and one left early. Steve, Marilyn, and their two allies were very disappointed. They had expected that at least a dozen leaders would attend and had prepared for as many as fifteen to eighteen.

"Maybe it was the weather," suggested Steve late that afternoon. "This really has been too nice a day to be cooped up in one room for seven or eight hours. Maybe we should have picked a November or January date when the weather would not be such strong competition."

"No, I don't think it was the weather," corrected a thirty-five-year-old person who had been one of the four who had planned this event. "I've been in this church all my life, and I don't believe the folks here understood what this was all about. Steve and Marilyn wanted us to talk about a three-year plan and I can appreciate the value of that, but I don't believe the people here think that way. I believe the folks here are used to planning on a two or three month basis. For example, we never begin to plan for our vacation Bible school that is held every June until sometime after Easter, and we usually don't start to plan the Christmas program until after school has started in the fall. I believe the reason so few turned out today was because they weren't comfortable with what we were proposing."

This experience illustrates another difference between small-membership churches and large congregations. The smaller the membership, the shorter the time frame for planning. The larger the membership, the longer that time frame for program planning. Steve had served his post-seminary apprenticeship in a very large church and had learned the value of long-range program planning. When he accepted a call to Bethany Church, he brought that learned value with him, but (except for Marilyn Barrett) he found very few members who supported the idea of a long time frame for planning. Smaller churches, as Karl Spencer had discovered when it came to church finances, tend to operate on a short time frame.

"What does your minister do best?" asked the staff member from denominational headquarters as he interviewed various members of the 847-member First Church. This was one of several questions he was asking individuals and small groups in preparation for an all-day Saturday planning retreat.

The most frequent responses he heard were, "Preaching," "Administration," "Sermons," "Teacher," "Leading Worship," and "Organizer."

Several weeks later, this same denominational staff person followed the same procedure in preparation for an evening meeting with the Board of the 217-member Maple Hill Church. He spent most of that day visiting members. Among the questions he asked them was, "What does your pastor do best as a minister?"

The most frequently offered responses were, "He loves every one of us." "He cares!" "He has made a point to get around and get acquainted with everyone." "He always has a good word for everyone." "He really fits in here better than any minister we've had in a long time." "He's only been here a little while, but he knows everyone by name, including all the kids."

When members of the large church are asked to appraise the strengths of their pastor, they tend to concentrate on the functional dimensions of the office. By contrast, when members of small churches are asked the same question, many of them tend to emphasize the relational dimensions of the person.

Some readers may question whether this pattern reflects a difference between small-membership churches and large congregations, or whether the difference in responses represents the fact that smaller congregations tend to be served by pastors who emphasize interpersonal relationships, and large congregations tend to be served by ministers who specialize in functional competence. The answer to that question may be, "both." Or it may be that smaller congregations emphasize the relational dimensions of life and thus use that criterion in seeking a pastor, while large churches focus on the functions of ministry and stress that yardstick in searching for a minister.

"They taught us in seminary that a church had to receive enough new members each year to be equal to six to eight percent of the membership or the congregation would decline in size," reflected Margaret Brandt, who was in her fourth year as the pastor of a 214-member church. She was spending the day with her closest friend from seminary, Louise Anderson. Louise was in her fourth year as the associate minister of the 1438-member Central Church.

"That was a lot of baloney!" replied Louise. "The senior minister here at Central and I sat down last January and figured it out. Last year we received 131 new members, including 87 who came by letter of transfer. That's more than 9 percent, yet we showed a net loss of seventeen. We figured we have to receive new members equal to at least 10 percent of our membership to stay on a plateau, and about 11 or 12 percent a year to show any net growth. That's a lot of people to meet and get acquainted with in one year!"

"That's strange," replied Margaret. "Last year we received fifteen new members. That's almost exactly equal to 7 percent of our total membership, but we showed a net increase of seven. The year before, we received fourteen new members and reported a net increase of five. The year before that, we received seventeen new members and had a net gain of nine. My people are delighted that our church is growing. We're now over two hundred members for the first time in the church's history. Maybe you have a higher turnover of the population here in this community?"

This conversation reflects one of the most subtle and difficult-to-measure differences between large congregations and smaller ones. The basic generalization is that the larger the membership of a congregation, the faster it must run to hold even.

A more precise statement is that the larger the membership figure, the higher the "dropout" rate.

In broad general terms, congregations lose members through four routes—deaths, transfers out, dropouts, and expulsions. In Protestant congregations in the United States and Canada, the death rate averages 1.2 deaths per 100 members per year. The losses by transfers to other congregations average approximately 2.8 persons per 100 members annually. In the small-membership church, the number of "dropouts"—the people who drop out but do not transfer their membership to another congregation—average only one or two per year per 100 members. In large congregations, the dropout rate often approaches 5 or 6 percent annually. That is one of the most significant differences between small-membership churches and most larger congregations. For a variety of reasons, the dropout problem is more serious in larger churches.

A. How Is It Different?

These examples illustrate the central thesis of this book. The small-membership congregation is a different *type* of religious institution than the larger churches. Before moving on to a discussion of why this is such a critical factor in planning for the life, ministry, outreach, and program of the small-membership church, it may be useful to review some of the other differences that set the small church apart as a distinctive component of the institutional expression of Christ's universal Church. To underscore this point, it may help to lift up a score of these differences. It should be emphasized that not every distinction applies to every congregation. Frequently these differences may be overshadowed by nationality, ethnic, racial, and denominational differences, or by local traditions.

1. The small church is tough! While some may argue this should not be at the top of the list, one of the most distinctive characteristics of the small church is that it is a hardy institution that usually can survive a succession of disasters. By contrast, the large church is often fragile and highly vulnerable to either external or internal erosion.

2. The long-established Anglo church is usually built around a ministry of the laity. The overwhelming majority of small-membership congregations on the North American continent are "owned and operated" by the laity. By contrast, the decision-making processes in large churches tend to be dominated by the clergy. Persons who are interested in seeing an operational implementation of the concept of the ministry of the laity will find it most easily by visiting small congregations. In thousands of small congregations there are no seminary-trained and ordained ministers on the scene. Even in those small-membership churches served by a seminary-trained minister, the pastor usually has less influence in charting the course than is true in the large congregations.

There are three overlapping exceptions to this generalization that must be identified. The first, and most common, exception is the relatively new congregation that is still served by the original pastor. Frequently, these congregations have been built around the personality of that founding pastor, and the laity have a secondary role.

The second exception is black churches. Regardless of how long they have been in existence, black congregations frequently are strongly pastor-centered. The name and personality of the pastor constitute the central core of the identity of thousands of black churches.

The third exception to this generalization is the congregation that, regardless of size, is (a) located at either the very conservative or the very liberal end of the theological spectrum, and (b) is either an "independent" congregation or has a very loose denominational affiliation. Regardless of age, size, or ethnic character, these congregations often are very pastor-centered, with the laity in a supportive role to that strong and magnetic ministerial personality.

3. The small church is a volunteer organization. The typical small-membership congregation is far more dependent on lay volunteers than is the large church. This distinction can be seen in the choir director, in the pianist or organist, in the people who carry out the janitorial duties, in the maintenance of the real estate, in the calling on the sick and shut-ins, in the teaching ministry, in the keeping of the financial records, in the care of the babies in the nursery, and in staffing the youth program. In dozens of areas in which the large churches often rely on paid staff members, the small churches usually turn to lay volunteers.

4. The small church cares more for people than for performance. The large church often employs specialists, such as lead singers in the choir, in its emphasis on quality in performance. This often appears strange to persons from small churches in which the emphasis is on people volunteering for ministry rather than on the quality of performance. In somewhat oversimplified terms, the smaller churches have a higher tolerance for unevenness in

performance and thus are more willing to rely on unpaid volunteers rather than turn to expensive specialists.

5. The small church rewards generalists. The large churches tend to expect both paid staff members and lay volunteers to possess and display specialized skills.

In the small church, however, the premium is on generalists. This includes the preacher who can finish cement, the Sunday school superintendent who can lead group singing, the president of the women's organization who can repair inoperative plumbing, and the church treasurer who can teach the high school Sunday school class.

6. The grapevine is an asset in the small church. The generalization that goes with this distinction is that the larger the size of the membership and/or the more complex the community setting, the more likely that the grapevine will carry more erroneous messages than accurate bits of information. Thus the small, rural church in a sparsely populated county often can depend on the grapevine, while the large city church must publish a weekly newsletter.

7. The small church has a different system for the financial support of the congregation. This point was illustrated in the opening section of this chapter. In many small-membership churches, the members contribute in response to what are the perceived needs of that congregation. In large churches, it is far more difficult for all members to fully comprehend both the scale and the variety of the financial needs of that congregation, so a different system must be developed to underwrite the financial base of that large and complex organization.

8. The small church is intergenerational. Most human beings tend to be more comfortable associating with people from the same age cohort. This natural tendency can be seen among preschool children, teenagers, young couples, mature widows, and dozens of other social groupings. In the larger congregations, where there often are several

members from any one slice of the age mix, social groups tend to form around age. By contrast, in many small churches, the dynamics of congregational life naturally tend to bring people together in repeated face-to-face contacts across generational lines.

One of the most significant implications of this generalization is that the small rural church, along with the conservation movement, is one of the few places in American society in which the concept of intergenerational obligation is being perpetuated. For the rest of society the operational principle is that each generation looks after its own interests, rather than being concerned about the plight of past or future generations.

9. The small church is relational. "Who was that?" asked Larry Brown of his wife after they had chatted briefly with another member of the large First Church. "Oh, don't you know her?" replied Mary Brown, "That's the new president of the women's organization here."

"Who was that?" asked Mrs. Smith of her forty-seven-year-old daughter. Mrs. Smith was visiting her daughter and son-in-law who had just moved to a rural community in northern Alabama, and she had accompanied them to church on this Sunday morning. "Oh, I guess I didn't say her name very clearly," replied the daughter. "That is Marlys Jackson. She and her husband are the parents of the two teenagers who sat directly in front of us this morning. Her husband is the tall man I introduced you to when we arrived this morning. Their oldest daughter is studying to be a minister."

In the large congregation, there is a tendency for people to conceptualize reality in terms of functional categories, whether it be in describing the greatest competence of the pastor, in categorizing people, in designing the organizational structure for the congregation, or in evaluating the performance of that congregation.

By contrast, in small congregations the members tend to think in terms of interpersonal relationships. The relationships of life, rather than the functions of the church, top the priority list in the small church.

10. The small church uses an internal clock. "What time do you begin the Sunday morning worship service here?" In the small congregation the reply might be, "As soon as the minister gets here. You see, she conducts an earlier service at a church eight miles east of here," or "Whenever the choir is ready," or "When everyone is here," or "About 10:30," or "About 11:00."

In general terms, the larger the number of people involved, the greater the informal pressure on the leadership to adhere to the external clock very carefully. The smaller the number of people involved, the greater the freedom the people have in following their own personal pace rather than letting the clock run the schedule.

11. The small church follows a different calendar. There is a growing trend among pastors of large congregations to adhere very closely to the liturgical year. In addition, an increasing number of large churches have decided to follow the same Sunday morning schedule for every Sunday of the year. This often is very difficult in some churches, such as in parts of the Sunbelt where the Sunday morning worship attendance may average over 500 in January and drop to less than 100 in August, but many larger congregations have concluded that the predictability of the same schedule is preferable to the confusion of changing it twice a year.

In a Wisconsin farming community, the pastor greeted a parishioner one spring morning, "Well, Fred, I see it's warm enough to let the cows out." This pastor knew that several of the men in the congregation had to clean the dairy barn seven mornings a week, and during the winter months, that took most of the morning. When Fred showed up for the 9:00 A.M. worship service that Sunday morning, the pastor knew it was warm enough to let the cows out after milking. That meant Fred, who was an excellent dairy farmer, could make it to church by nine o'clock.

The calendar in the small church not only is greatly influenced by the seasons of the year, it also is heavily influenced by family reunions, language and nationality differences, ethnic customs, community events, and congregational traditions.

This generalization has its greatest application to (a) rural congregations, (b) nationality churches, (c) black churches, and (d) congregations composed of recent immigrants to the United States.

12. The small church has a place for everyone! In recent years thousands of large urban churches have become very self-conscious about the fact they tend to exclude single adults. A much smaller number have made a serious effort to reach the physically handicapped, the mentally retarded, and other people who may feel excluded.

To some members who have spent their entire life in a small congregation, these efforts appear somewhat unreal. As long as they can remember, Evelyn, who is regarded as a little "slow," has always been a part of the fellowship of that small church. Likewise, for years, Helen, who never married, has been one of the four or five hardest workers in that same congregation. Joe, who also has been single for all of his sixty-seven years, has been the respected and trusted church treasurer for twenty-two years. Every Sunday, three men surround Emma's wheelchair and carry it up the steps to the sanctuary. No one has ever asked why every Sunday, Frank, who is completely deaf, is in the same pew he has occupied for over sixty years. A few people joke about Harold, who cannot carry a tune, being the senior member of the choir. Darlene, who is thirty-seven and single, is the new chairperson of the Board. Why would a church have to develop specialized ministries for singles or for the mentally retarded?

One of the most significant characteristics of thousands of small congregations is that they accept people who might feel rejected in a much larger congregation. Some of these are accepted because they have good bloodlines. Others are accepted and included because of their willingness to help with any job. A few gained complete acceptance several decades ago, before their current affliction impaired their ability to be an active participant. Every one of them, however, has good friends in that congregation. Every one feels needed. Every one knows that if he or she is absent, the rest will notice that vacant place and miss the one who regularly occupied it. Every one is assured that when he or she dies, there will be a big crowd at the funeral service.

13. Kinfolk ties are more important in the small church. What does it mean if there are twenty-nine people in this congregation who are related to you by blood or by marriage?

In the 960-member church, that is 3 percent of the membership and probably will not be a major factor in congregational life. In the 87-member congregation, that is one-third of the membership and almost certainly will mean those kinship ties will have a tremendous influence on the life of that church.

In addition, the intimacy of the fellowship and the impact of kinship ties may mean that a new baby will be baptized in the small church shortly after birth because the grandparents insist on it. If those same young parents had moved to another part of the country three years earlier, that new baby might not be baptized, since both sets of grandparents are over a thousand miles away.

The pressure of kinship ties also is one reason why the "dropout rate" is often lower in the small church than in the large congregation.

Kinship ties are also influential in the selection of officers, in the alignment of opposing sides when a controversial issue surfaces, and in maintaining certain customs and traditions.

14. Individuals, not committees, often do the work in small churches. "Why don't we refer that to the music committee?" suggests a leader at the board meeting of the 700-member church. "I think that is the responsibility of the evangelism committee," suggests someone else a half hour later, when another issue is raised.

"I'll be seeing Martha in the morning, and I'll ask her if she will take care of that," offers someone at the board meeting of the 63-member church. A few minutes later, someone else says, "This afternoon Harold told me that he couldn't be here tonight but that he would see that the piano is tuned before we start rehearsing for the Christmas program."

These comments reflect the tendency in large churches to refer matters to committees, while in smaller congregations a greater dependence is placed on individuals—and that is the appropriate way to do it! (A common mistake in many large congregations is to try to operate as if they were a small church. That method has proved to be one of the most effective means of turning a large congregation into a middle-sized church.)

In broad general terms, larger congregations tend to function around an organizational structure that places heavy responsibilities on committees, while smaller churches tend to delegate responsibilities to individuals.

One result of this is that in the larger churches there is a strong tendency for the governing board to set policy and to delegate to committees the authority and responsibility for detailed program and administrative concerns.

By contrast, in thousands of smaller congregations, and in too many middle-sized churches, the governing board functions as a committee of the whole, with individual members of that body taking responsibility for the follow-up action on specific concerns.

15. The small church often is a participatory democracy. This is a complementary reflection on the previous distinction. Small congregations tend to resemble a participatory democracy, while larger churches must function along the lines of a representative system of church government.

It should be noted that there are significant denominational differences on this point. Presbyterians (with the exception of Cumberland Presbyterians) tend to emphasize a representative system of government; while the Quakers, Baptists, and many others encourage a participatory democracy with the final authority vested in the congregational meeting. Despite the polity differences, however, small churches tend to be heavily congregational in decision making, while larger churches tend to place the central authority in a small number of leaders. (In black congregations it is not unusual, regardless of size, for most of the authority to be vested in the minister.)

16. Social meetings dominate the agenda in the small church. "Our board meetings usually begin about 7:30 in the evening, and we go home about 10:30 or 11:00," explained Helen Jones, a long-time member of a 133-member congregation, to her cousin.

"Why in the world does it take so long in such a little church?" asked the cousin. "I'm on the board here at Central Church and our minister begins promptly at 8:00, and we're always done before 10:00. What kind of an agenda do you have in your church that takes so long?"

"Oh, we have about a three-hour social meeting every month that we interrupt every once in a while with some church business," explained Helen. "My husband claims we have two hours of fellowship and one hour of business, and that's why it takes three hours every month for our board meeting."

Helen has identified one of the two central reasons why board meetings in smaller churches often drag on for two, three, or four hours. One reason is that considerable time is spent on the fellowship needs of the members. The other reason was identified earlier. In the typical long-established small congregation, the governing board often functions as a committee of the whole and concentrates on details, rather than limiting itself to broad policy questions. (It must be added that in many larger congregations, the governing board functions as if it were part of a small church.)

17. The small church is easier to comprehend. One of the most subtle, but very influential, distinctions among churches, when looked at according to size, is how much time a person has to invest in order to be aware of all facets of congregational life and ministry.

In the typical small-membership congregation, a member can invest an average of four to six hours a week and be reasonably well informed about nearly every aspect of that congregation's life and ministry, including the present condition of most of the members.

In the middle-sized congregation, that investment of time increases to eight to fifteen hours a week for the well-informed member. In the very large congregation, it would require one hundred to two hundred hours a week to keep up-to-date on all aspects of congregational life. One result is that, in the very large churches, the senior minister and other paid staff members are always receiving surprises in the form of "news" that others thought they were aware of, but they had yet to hear.

Among the many implications of this distinction are (a) it is easier to be an influential lay leader in a smaller church than in a large congregation, (b) this is one of the less visible reasons behind the resistance to numerical growth in small membership churches, and (c) the grapevine is more reliable in the smaller churches than in larger congregations.

18. A majority of small churches are subsidized. While this is a subject many people like to avoid, the vast majority of small membership congregations currently are not paying their way. This is especially widespread among smaller and middle-sized city churches, but the pattern is not limited to the urban scene.

The most common form of indirect subsidy is received by the congregation that meets in a building constructed and paid for by a previous generation of members. The building is usually located on a parcel of land that also was paid for by a previous generation of church members. In a majority of these congregations, a part of the compensation for the minister is free use of a house that also was paid for by a previous generation of members. If today's members had to pay the full economic rent for the use of all that real estate provided by previous generations, it would mean a 15 to 40 percent increase in their current level of expenditures.

A second indirect subsidy to small churches that is more common in some denominations, such as The United Methodist and the Episcopal Church, is that small churches often are not expected to pay their share of the cost of various denominational programs. Examples include the salaries of staff, ministerial placement, denominationally supplied resources, health insurance and other benefits for the clergy, and the cost of operating the entire denominational structure; including theological seminaries, missions, and continuing education events. There is a widespread expectation that large congregations will pick up a disproportionately large share of these costs.

In some denominations, such as the Episcopal Church, the Presbyterian Church in the United States, The United Methodist Church and a few others, millions of dollars from denominational treasuries are allocated every year for the direct financial assistance of small congregations. These subsidies may be granted as salary supplement for the minister, program aid, loans at below-market-interest rates, grants for maintenance or expansion of the building, or as emergency aid.

The rebuttal is often made that large churches *should* provide some financial help to smaller churches, because (a) the small churches supply training experiences for the future pastors of the large churches, (b) the small church transfers more members to big congregations than they receive by transfer from the larger churches, (c) the churches with more resources should help those with limited resources (Acts 4:32–5:10), (d) the large churches are ones that benefit most from the availability of denominational resources, and (e) most missionary ventures, specialized ministries, and supplemental benefits for the clergy were created at the instigation of people from the larger churches; therefore it is only right that the larger congregations should pay most of the costs.

Regardless of where the reader stands on the merits of that debate, one of the distinctive characteristics of many smaller churches, as well as a substantial number of middle-sized and larger congregations, is that today's generation of members may not be paying the full cost of today's operation.

Some lay persons married to a pastor will add that many small churches are subsidized by the pastor's spouse—but that is not unique to the small church!

19. The small church tends to rely on an "attraction" model in new-member recruitment. In broad general terms, there are two New Testament models for reaching people outside the church.[2] Some churches seek to attract potential new members who will take the initiative in making contact with that congregation. The bulletin board in the front yard

with the weekly schedule on it, or an advertisement on the religion page of the newspaper are examples of a passive approach to attracting newcomers.

Other congregations actively go out and proclaim the gospel and confront people with the fact that Jesus Christ is Lord and Savior. This active proclamation effort may take the form of visiting people in prison, a systematic visitation-evangelism program, establishing a Sunday school in a storefront to reach unchurched people, launching a specialized ministry to reach and serve families that include a Downs Syndrome child, or setting aside 5 percent of the budget for direct-mail evangelism.

Smaller congregations tend to seek to grow by following the attraction model, while the proclamation approach is usually found in larger congregations. (One reason behind this generalization is that the proclamation method is far more effective in reaching people outside any worshiping congregation than is the attraction model. Thus, when small congregations utilize the proclamation model, they often cease to be small churches.)

20. The piano often is the central musical instrument in the small church. The piano possesses several distinctive advantages as a musical instrument in worship. These include: (a) it is usually easier to find someone competent to play a piano than it is to find a skilled organist, (b) many choir members find it easier to sing when accompanied by a piano than when accompanied by an organ or an orchestra, (c) in most church buildings the congregation can hear itself sing better when the musical instrument is a piano rather than an organ, (d) a piano often has a greater "integrity of sound" in a small building than does an organ that is not designed for that building, (e) more people have experience singing with a piano than with an organ, and (f) in recent years there has been a significant increase in materials available for use with a vocal group accompanied by a piano.

This means the small-membership church probably should not attempt to copy the music program of a larger congregation that has a pipe organ, a handbell choir and perhaps a brass instrumental group. In other words, the ministry of music in the typical small-membership congregation probably should be tailored to a piano, not an organ. This may meet considerable resistance from some members of today's 134-member congregation that meets in a building designed to house 400 at worship and includes an excellent pipe organ that was given as a memorial several years ago.

B. What Are the Implications?

At this point, the reader may be asking, "So what? Those are interesting observations, but what is the relevance to the small-membership church?" That is a fair question. The basic response is that, since the small-membership church is *not* a small-scale model of larger congregations, all plans for the ministry, program, and administration of these congregations should be designed in response to the distinctive characteristics of the smaller church. The mother making a dress for her six-year-old daughter will run into difficulties if she uses a dress pattern for her own size and attempts to scale it down to fit the daughter. She will have an easier task and produce a more attractive garment if she begins by picking out a pattern designed for her six-year-old daughter.

A parallel point can be made if one looks at the implications of the unique characteristics of the small church from four different perspectives.

C. From a Lay Perspective

The first perspective is that of the lay person with an active leadership role in a congregation with fewer than 75 to 100 people at worship on the average Sunday morning.

The Small Church Is Different!

Whether that person is serving on the committee to search for a new minister, as an usher on Sunday morning, or as a representative to a denominational program agency, it will help to remember the small church is different. Perhaps the best way to communicate this point is to offer three operational examples.

When looking for a pastor to replace the minister who resigned a few months ago, the crucial criteria for the pulpit committee from the small church are not educational attainment, oratorical ability, academic records, scholarly achievements, or experience on denominational committees. This committee usually is seeking a pastor who genuinely loves people, is an extroverted personality, really enjoys being with people, and is a walking model of an adult Christian.

Or, the primary responsibility of the usher in the small-membership church is not to hand people a copy of the bulletin and usher them to a pew. The most important obligations of that usher are to make each individual who walks in that door feel wanted, welcome, loved, respected, and needed.

Likewise, when serving on a denominational committee planning a training event for leaders and workers from small congregations, the small-church representative may have to remind the others that the key criteria for selecting the place to host that event are not a central location, adequate offstreet parking, the capability to serve a meal to a large number of people in a short period of time, or the quality of the meeting rooms. The most important single criterion in selecting a meeting place for a training event for people from small churches is to avoid intimidating them. Every possible effort should be made to avoid the possibility that the people attending that event will be overwhelmed by the resources available at the big First Church, and go home saying to one another, "Golly, we could *never* do that!" A better goal is to schedule the event in a place that will encourage those attending to leave saying to one another, "If they can do that here, we should be able to do it back in our church, since we have more resources than they have here."

D. From the Pastoral Perspective

A second person who will find it useful to affirm the fact that small congregations are not miniaturized versions of large churches is the pastor.

Conventional wisdom suggests that most ministers were reared in small rural churches, so they all have first-hand knowledge of the distinctive characteristics of these congregations. The facts do not support that assumption. For many years now, ministers have been coming in disproportionately large numbers from larger churches located in urban counties. The Presbyterian Church in the United States, for example, reports that, as of December 1979, only 7 percent of all ministerial candidates came from congregations with fewer than one hundred members, and 52 percent came from congregations with over 500 members, despite the fact that the congregations with fewer than a hundred members account for 9 percent of the members of that denomination, and the churches with over 500 members include only 49 percent of all members.[3] A simple translation of those numbers is that there is one chance in fourteen that the new minister coming directly from seminary to a Presbyterian church grew up in a church with fewer than a hundred members, and a fifty-fifty chance that the recent seminary graduate came from a congregation with more than 500 members.

Among the operational implications for the pastor of the small-membership church are these six guidelines.

The Small Church Is Different!

1. Relationships with people are more important than the functions of ministry.

2. Kinfolk ties are important, the grapevine does work, and people do repeat comments they hear about their friends and relatives.

3. The smaller the size of the membership, the less privacy that is automatically accorded the minister and the members of the minister's household.

4. In the large congregation, most of the members expect the minister to be *the* leader, but in small congregations the members expect the pastor will be one of several leaders, and not necessarily the most influential member of that leadership team.

5. In the small congregation, it is tempting for the newly arrived pastor to set a pace that exceeds the available resources and the number of workers.

6. The large-membership church needs a pastor who is skilled in working with large groups, while the small-membership church often requires its pastor to have a high level of competence in affirming and utilizing the values of small face-to-face groups.[4]

When translated into day-to-day terms, these guidelines suggest the minister serving the small congregation should be comfortable with unscheduled interruptions, remember that every conversation and meeting may involve relatives of the person involved, be hesitant to make unilateral changes in the format of the Christmas Eve service, learn to be comfortable with less than the ideal degree of privacy, set goals that can be achieved with the available resources, be careful not to "overload the agenda" at the monthly board meeting to the point that the time for fellowship is eliminated, express surprise and delight when told that the Tuesday afternoon women's circle had seven in attendance last week, and design a youth program that does not require fifteen or twenty participants in order to function satisfactorily.

E. From a Denominational Perspective

One of the concepts that had a very negative impact on the United States Army in Vietnam was the declaration that "every second lieutenant is a potential future chief of staff."[5] A parallel concept that can be equally destructive is for denominational leaders to perceive every small congregation as a future thousand-member church. As was pointed out earlier, a very persuasive case can be made for the thesis that the normative size for a Protestant congregation on the North American continent is the church with 30 to 40 people at worship on the average Sunday morning. To produce congregations larger than that is like pumping water uphill. It can be done, but it means opposing the forces of nature and requires persistent and continuous effort.

Denominational staff members can be more effective in their relationships with small-membership churches if they are always conscious of the fact that smaller congregations have a distinctive set of internal dynamics that make them function differently.

In working with small congregations, it may help the outsider to remember the following. (a) The laity see the central threads of continuity as being in the congregation and in the meeting place, not in the minister, or even in the denominational affiliation. (b) The members tend to place a higher value on the personal characteristics of the minister than on his or her professional competence. (c) The small church tends to use a shorter time frame in planning and scheduling than does the denomination, but these members expect the denomination to use at least a two-year time frame for scheduling major denominational events. (d) The members often use a different conceptual framework for looking at church finances than that advocated by denominational leaders. (e) The basis for authority in the

small church is personal and direct, while in the denominational structure it tends to be bureaucratic, contractual,
and vested in the office—thus the denominational leaders
who are most effective in working with people from smaller
congregations are those officials who personally earn the
support of people rather than expect it to be accorded them
by virtue of their office. (f) The social and the fellowship
dimensions of every gathering in the small church should
be strongly affirmed by any visitor. (g) The decision-making
processes in the small-membership church tend to be less
structured and more informal than recommended in the
manual on denominational policy. (h) Many of the
denominationally initiated programs and procedures that
have been developed for the benefit of middle-sized and
larger congregations are not appropriate for small churches,
and some may even be counterproductive if forced on these
churches.

The small-membership church functions by a different set
of organizing principles than those of the large church. The
"glue" that produces a sense of unity and cohesiveness in
the small-membership churches is not the same as the
unifying principles that constitute the central organizing
principles of the very large congregation.[6]

F. From a Parish Perspective

A fourth perspective for looking at the application of the
implications of the unique character of the small-membership church is from that of the congregation itself.

Instead of seeking to copy the style of ministry of larger
congregations or yielding to the pressures to fit into a
pattern developed for other churches, the small congregation should affirm its own distinctive character.

What, for example, should be the response when
someone in the 89-member congregation, meeting in a

small building, suggests that memorial gifts should be accumulated to purchase an electronic organ? It might be appropriate for a long-time member to ask, "Considering the size of the building and the nature of our membership, wouldn't it be better to spend that money on a really good piano?"

What should be the response when the recently arrived minister suggests to the 127-member church that it is necessary to expand the committee structure? It might be helpful for someone to respond, "We usually can handle all the business we have through the board, the trustees and the Christian education committee; why should we overload our people with more meetings?"

What should be the response in the small church when someone from a denominational committee suggests this 47-member congregation should merge with that 81-member church in order to reduce the cost of maintaining two separate meeting places? Someone might ask, "Do you believe the federal government should cut down and sell those giant redwood trees in Muir Woods in order to balance the national budget? Do you believe the Washington Monument should be closed in order to reduce governmental expenditures? This building is a sacred place for many of us. The funeral service for Helen's husband was held here. All three of our daughters were married here. My wife was baptized and confirmed in this building. My brother accepted Jesus Christ as Lord and Savior here one night. This building is filled with hallowed memories for many of us. Does it make sense for us to surrender this sacred place in order to save a few dollars?"

What happens when someone suggests combining our Sunday school with that of the church across the street in order to have enough children to change to a closely graded church school? Someone might point out, "Please remember that our intergenerational character is one of the unique advantages of this church. Perhaps we should think twice before we sacrifice that in favor of bigger numbers."

What should be the response when someone points out that, in last year's renovation project, three times as much money was spent on modernizing the kitchen as was spent on remodeling the chancel? Perhaps an appropriate reply would be, "You must remember that we're not simply a collection of individuals. A small church such as this one really is a family. When the family eats together, those family ties are reinforced. The kitchen is a very important room in your home, and the kitchen is a very important room in the church home of the small congregation. The more we stress our self-image as a family, the more important is that kitchen!"

The members of the small church should not be hesitant about lifting up and affirming their distinctive characteristics and the unique personality of their congregation.[7] After these assets are identified, and after the implications are widely recognized, it will be easier to begin a constructive conversation on alternative methods of strengthening, reinforcing, and expanding the ministry and outreach of that congregation.

G. Commitment in the Small Church

"We wouldn't have all these problems if our members were more committed," exclaimed Mrs. Hanson. Her comment was aroused by a discussion of some of the problems facing the 157-member St. James Church.

The list included a leveling off in membership growth, an increasingly acute financial squeeze, the shrinking church school, the drop off in attendance at Sunday morning worship, and the difficulty in enlisting volunteers to accept leadership positions in the parish.

"You're right," agreed Jim Martin, "but how do we get

people to be more committed? If we could get all the members of St. James to take their membership vows seriously, we wouldn't have any problems. But how do we raise the level of commitment?"

There are at least three facets to a comprehensive response to Jim Martin's question. Each one merits the careful attention of leaders who are concerned about what appears to be the low commitment level of some of the members. The first of these is to stand back and take a larger view of that term *commitment*.

While not every reader will be happy with this, from a simple descriptive point of view there are at least two expressions of commitment. Some people are committed to Jesus Christ as Lord and Savior and also have a very strong commitment to the life, ministry, program, and outreach of a particular worshiping congregation.

There are also many people in this world who accept Jesus Christ as Lord, but who are not actively involved in the life of any worshiping congregation. Most social surveys on this subject indicate that, in the United States, for every ten members carried on the membership rolls of the congregation in any of the larger Protestant denominational families, there are four more people, age 18 and over, who identify themselves as members of churches in that denomination. In other words, the number of self-identified Christians (churched and unchurched) is far larger than the combined membership of all the churches in the United States. Many declare a commitment to Christ, but they do not feel the need to display any commitment to a specific congregation. Some of these people have been "burned out" by an unhappy experience in a church. Others have been exhausted by being overworked. Many have been "confirmed" as members, but never have been assimilated into the fellowship of any congregation.

In simple terms, it appears that tens of thousands of

The Small Church Is Different!

Americans make an operational distinction between a commitment to Jesus Christ as Lord and Savior and a commitment to the institutional expression of the universal church that we identify as the worshiping congregation.

The other side of the picture can be seen in those people who do not openly profess any Christian commitment, but are greatly disturbed when they hear someone talking about the possibility that small church down the road or across the street may close.

While it is not necessary to accept this distinction between a commitment to Christ and a commitment to a specific worshiping congregation as good, valid, or consistent with the Christian tradition, it is important to ask, "Does this appear to be an accurate description of reality?"

If it is (and this writer obviously believes it is), we can go on and examine a second facet of the response to Jim Martin's question.

Why do people feel a commitment or strong sense of loyalty to an organization? The commitment of most loyal and active members of nearly every organization can be placed in one of two categories. These two categories provide a beginning point for developing a response to the question of raising the level of individual commitment.

In some congregations, and especially in smaller churches established several decades ago, the commitment of many of the loyal and active members appears to be based to a very substantial degree on a heritage shared by many members of the congregation.

This fellowship includes some, but not necessarily all, of the members who have spent a large proportion of their adult life as members of the same congregation, and/or those who have not spent many years as active members of other congregations. It also may include some of the adult offspring of members.

In a typical example of this pattern, let us look at one

congregation that was established more than fifty years ago. Many of the active adult members of today have been in this congregation for at least three decades, and only a small proportion of the older adults have spent as many of their adult years in another congregation as they have in this one.

These members have in common many of the same roots in this congregation. They have shared many responsibilities. They have been through "good" and "bad" times together. They have been very close to one another and have a strong attachment to this congregation.

In many such churches, most of the older members share the same nationality, race, subculture, socio-economic-educational, language, and/or theological characteristics.

In a decreasing number of congregations this shared heritage is based on a deep denominational loyalty and is expressed in an active commitment to whatever parish the person happens to belong at that time. This strong denominational loyalty still can be seen in many Lutherans, Episcopalians, Baptists, Presbyterians, and United Methodists, as well as in members of smaller denominations.

The other most frequently encountered expression of active commitment by individuals to a particular congregation is in shared contemporary goals. These active members tend to focus their conversation "about our church" on what is happening now. This emphasis on shared contemporary goals often is expressed in such comments as the following:

"It looks as if we'll be able to move into the new building in another month."

"Our weekday nursery school now has over 30 children."

"We raised more than $3,000 last Sunday in the special offering for world hunger."

"We have more than 50 trained laypersons in our visitation evangelism program."

"Our Lay Witness Mission is scheduled for next month."

"Let me tell you what's happening in our new Bible study group."

"We helped launch the planned parenthood clinic that is housed in our building."

In each case, the commitment to the congregation includes a contemporary goal that has meaning to that member, and that also offers an opportunity for that member to find meaning and fulfillment.

This distinction between "heritage" or "shared roots" as the source of the institutional commitment for some members and "contemporary goals" as the basis for the commitment of others is of crucial importance for leaders in small-membership congregations. If the goal is to enlist and motivate lay volunteers who have been long-time members of that congregation, it may be wise to emphasize the shared roots source of institutional commitment.

On the other hand, if the effort is directed at enlisting lay volunteers from among new members, and others who do not share in this heritage from earlier days, it may be wise to focus on the excitement and meaning of these new goals in ministry.

This distinction also may be useful in understanding the alienation and occasional withdrawal of some of the "oldtimers" when new members suggest new goals that appear to threaten the local heritage.

The third facet of a response to Jim Martin's question concerns the nature of the commitment of the members of the long-established small church. In addition to religious commitment, many members of the long-established small congregations display a strong commitment to (a) each other; (b) that meeting place; (c) kinfolk ties; (d) the concept that a church should resemble a larger, closely knit, intergenerational, harmonious, and caring family; (e) the women's organization and its goals; (f) local traditions and customs; (g) the Sunday church school; and (h) in a minority of small-membership congregations, the church-owned cemetery.

By contrast, in larger congregations, more members display a stronger commitment to (a) the minister; (b) specific programs, ministries, and subgroups such as an adult class, a prayer circle, a committee, or a local cause (such as social action or the weekday preschool program); (c) the denomination; and/or (d) specific mission efforts (such as a children's home, a foreign mission field, a church-related college, or a home for the elderly).

While this subtle distinction among various expressions of institutional commitment will be of little interest to perhaps nine out of ten church members, there are several significant implications for four groups of individuals. These are (a) the recently arrived minister who is serving a small-membership church, (b) the leaders in these congregations who have a deep, but realistic interest in numerical growth, (c) denominational staff people with responsibilities for small-membership churches, and (d) lay persons who have transferred their membership from a larger congregation to a small-membership church.

In operational terms, these implications can be divided into three categories.

First, the strong commitment of the members to one another, to kinfolk ties, to the meeting place, to the concept that the congregation should function as one big family, and the modest emphasis on program tend to reinforce the single-cell character of the small church. When combined with the intergenerational nature of the typical long-established small church, these forces tend to enhance the caring nature of the fellowship, but at the cost of potential numerical growth. These unifying principles tend to make the small church an exclusionary institution. While there usually is not a conscious effort to exclude strangers, these expressions of institutional commitment tend to make it difficult for the small-membership church to reach, attract, and assimilate potential new members, unless people have kinfolk in that congregation.

While this is very difficult for many people to accept, the more closely knit the fellowship ties of a congregation, the less likely it will be able to achieve significant numerical growth, unless there is a major effort to expand the total program.

Second, the role of the minister is affected by these forms of institutional commitment. With the exception of the minister who has served a decade or longer in the same church, this usually means the small-membership church does not provide a strong support group for the minister. On the other hand, in many small congregations the people feel free, and sometimes obligated to check up on the minister, but not necessarily in a supportive manner. This is a special source of complaint from many single women serving small churches!

Another consequence is that when the minister is caught between two factions in a large church, the divisive issue frequently can be identified in terms of mission, program, or a definition of the role of the church. In the small-membership church, the minister may be caught between opposing factions, but the divisive issue is often a local tradition or a family feud, and may have little to do with the mission or program of that church.

In many long-established small churches, the commitment to tradition, the emphasis on kinfolk ties, and the modest commitment to program may combine to severely limit the leadership role of the pastor. The minister is often expected to be a chaplain rather than an initiating leader.

The more the pastor is committed to contemporary goals in the congregation where most of the leader's institutional commitment grows out of shared roots and a common local heritage, the more likely it is that the minister will (a) feel inhibited by what appears to be an excessive amount of apathy, and/or (b) turn to new members for help in implementing new goals.

Closely related to this is the fact that, in the typical small-membership church, the minister is younger than the median age of the membership and often has a very strong future orientation. This may create a divisive gap in perspective in those congregations in which most of the leaders have a strong institutional commitment to shared roots out of the past. This divergence also may be one reason why pastors in small-membership churches express an above-average degree of interest in moving to another church.[8]

Finally, from an overall congregational perspective, these expressions of institutional commitment may (a) reduce the willingness to take an open approach to conflict resolution, (b) inhibit active support for innovations in program, (c) almost guarantee the success of any fund-raising effort to maintain the building (and the cemetery), but limit efforts to raise money for an expansion of program, (d) influence the selection of the criteria used in any effort at congregational self-evaluation, and (e) frustrate some efforts to expand the educational program beyond the Sunday school.

In the small-membership church, as in every other type of congregation, the values and attitudes of the members affect the life and ministry of that church. That is one reason why it is important to recognize that the small-membership church is not a small-scale version of larger congregations. It is different!

Recognizing the distinctive institutional character of the small church, rather than assuming that all congregations are basically the same regardless of size, may be the essential first step in any effort to strengthen, reinforce, and expand the ministry and outreach of over one half of the Protestant churches on this continent.

Chapter II

RESPONDING TO FOUR WIDESPREAD CONCERNS

hat do you see as the number-one issue confronting the small church during the last two decades of this century?" asked the leader of a weekend workshop for people from small-membership congregations.

"That's easy," quickly replied a man from an ex-neighborhood church in a city of a half million residents. "I can answer that with either one of two words. One is 'money.' The other 'inflation.' Take your pick, but that's the number-one issue we're faced with today. We're in a building that was designed for a thousand-member congregation, and I guess the church once had close to 1200 members, but now we're down to about two hundred members, and the cost of utilities and insurance plus the maintenance on the building takes more than a third of our budget."

"We've got financial problems, too," observed a woman from a small-town congregation, "but that is not the number-one issue. I think our most urgent problem is reaching and holding our young people. Everybody knows that the youth of today will be the church of tomorrow."

"For us, the number-one issue is self-image," declared a person from a small rural congregation. "Part of our problem is some country people tend to see themselves as inferior to city folks. When that feeling is reinforced by all the things the denomination does to perpetuate the idea that big churches are better than small ones, that simply reinforces the inferiority complex of the people in the small rural church. If we could afford our own minister, that might help, but we share a minister with two other churches."

"Those are all important issues," agreed a layman from a county seat town. "We're the smaller of the two churches from our denomination in a town with a population of nearly five thousand. The big First Church has had the same pastor now for twelve years. We've never had a minister who stayed more than four years, and four of the last six left in less than three years. I think the number-one issue facing the small church is getting and keeping good ministers. Maybe that's really a financial problem, as this gentleman has suggested, but I think there's more than money involved in getting and keeping a minister."

"I don't know about the rest of you, but I agree with this lady who spoke about the need to reach and keep the young people," declared an elderly man from a 94-member church. "We need more members, especially young ones, or we're going to die off. Last year we lost five members by death and two others moved into nursing homes. At that rate, it won't be long before we're out of business. I think the number-one problem is getting more members to keep our small churches going."

Money, morale, members, and ministerial leadership almost invariably appear near the top of the list when lay people from small churches are invited to voice their concerns about what the future may bring. In some denominational families, the Sunday school also is a source of concern. Frequently the concern about a stronger ministry with young people appears to be motivated as much by the fear that "our church is dying off" as by a desire to enhance the quality of the youth program.

Two of these six concerns—ministerial leadership and the Sunday school—are of such complexity that they merit separate chapters. The other four—morale, finances, church growth, and youth ministries—can be discussed here because they have one thing in common. A productive response requires an action agenda tailored to a particular issue and to that specific congregation.

A. Self-Esteem

If there is something approaching a universal beginning point for small-membership churches seeking to plan for tomorrow, it is strengthening the self-image.

There are at least seven factors behind the morale problems of many smaller congregations. First, the leaders in most congregations almost invariably underestimate the size, strength, resources, assets, and potential of that church. A simple illustration of this is that most of the members of the congregation averaging eighty at worship on Sunday morning are amazed to discover that that means they rank in the upper half in size among Protestant churches in the United States and Canada, if size is measured by attendance. A few are so convinced of the inferior status of their congregation they refuse to believe it. If the average attendance at the service is used to measure size, one half of all

CHURCH SIZE	
Average Attendance	Size
600	100 percentile
350	95 percentile
140	75 percentile
100	60 percentile
75	50 percentile
40	35 percentile
35	25 percentile
20	10 percentile
5	1 percentile

Protestant churches in the United States and Canada average fewer than seventy-five at worship, and a fourth average fewer than thirty-five at worship. This writer's experiences indicate that at least nineteen out of twenty congregational leaders underestimate the comparative size of the congregation of which they are members.

A second reason for the low level of self-esteem of many small-membership churches is a function of the human memory. All of us can recognize more than we can recall. Ask a person who was there to recall from memory and write down the names of the eighteen individuals who attended last night's meeting. Few will be able to do it. Give that same person a list of the names of the thirty persons who might have been present, with instructions to check off the names of the eighteen who actually attended. Most of us can do that.

In many small churches, it is assumed that everyone can recall, without any help, all of the ministries, programs, events, activities, victories, groups, and accomplishments of that congregation. Few of us can do that. We assume, however, that everyone can, and therefore conclude that it is unnecessary to recapture that whole package through a slide show, a series of posters, or some other comprehensive review that is more common in larger churches.

A third reason for the low morale in many congregations is they tend to follow a problem-based approach to planning. This planning model tends to reinforce gloom, pessimism, despair, and low self-esteem. A better approach is to begin the planning with the suggestion, "Let's build a list of the assets and strengths that are a product of our size, and then we can talk about how those can be foundation stones for strengthening, reinforcing, and expanding our ministry."

In one congregation this approach produced, in only a few minutes, this list of comments. "We know everyone by name." "We really care about one another." "We come to one another's assistance spontaneously, without the need for an elaborate system or structure." "We accept and affirm people who might feel rejected elsewhere." "We offer a strong adult male image to the children." "We're intergenerational." "We really do love one another." "We depend on each other, not on a minister." "Single adults are accepted without question here." "We can celebrate everyone's victories and share everyone's sorrows." "We're a lay-run church." "People respond when we're faced with a crisis."

That is a better beginning point for a planning meeting than to start by listing all the problems facing the congregation!

A fourth factor behind the low self-esteem of some congregations is that in several (but not all) denominational families, most of the seminary-trained ministers come out of larger churches, and a very large proportion of the denominational leaders come to that office from large churches. This naturally causes them to carry a large-church perspective into small churches.

Perhaps the most insidious factor is the operational assumption held in many (predominantly white and large, middle and upper-class) denominational families that small-membership churches must and should be subsidized by large churches. This concept is rarely encountered in congregations affiliated with the several black denominations. It also is rarely encountered in Hispanic congregations. Financial subsidies and high morale rarely go together!

A sixth factor on this list is the tenure of the minister. Nearly every change in ministers is disruptive. Therefore it would appear wise to minimize disruptions—that was the pattern in the Congregational churches in New England in the century between 1650 and 1750, when pastorates averaged nearly twenty-five years.[1]

In general, small-membership churches tend to be

strengthened when a period of several months elapses between the departure of one pastor and the arrival of the next minister. By contrast, frequent changes in ministers tend to be very disruptive. Every time the small church bids farewell to a minister who is moving on to a larger congregation, some of the members feel a sense of rejection. This tends to undercut the level of congregational self-esteem.

Perhaps even more subversive than the frequent changes in ministerial leadership is the retention of a pastor with low self-esteem, or one who has personal morale problems.

Finally, the leadership positions in some congregations that once were considerably larger in size than they are today, are filled by extremely articulate people with long memories, who cannot resist comparing today's situaton with "the good old days when Reverend Harrison was our minister." That condition may be the strongest single argument in favor of a mandatory policy of introducing new members into leadership positions. (In general terms, if more than one half of today's leaders have been members of this congregation for more than a dozen years, morale tends to be low. If more than one half of today's leaders have been members of this congregation for less than seven years, morale tends to be high.)

If the members of a church can diagnose the sources of low morale in that particular congregation, they will have taken the first essential step in treating that problem. An accurate diagnosis can be a very constructive step to a better future.

B. Youth Ministries

"I wish our church had enough money to hire a college student to come and be our youth director," exclaimed a frustrated Debbie Barzon to one of her friends in the High

Street Church. "The church I grew up in had thirty to forty kids in the youth program when I was in high school. Of course, that was a much larger church than this one is, but our assistant minister had the youth program as his number-one priority. Here, I guess when they have seven or eight kids out for the high school youth group, that's considered a crowd. Our Allison will be fourteen next year, and there's really nothing for her to look forward to here when she starts high school."

Mrs. Barzon's comments may evoke a sympathetic response, but they are not especially constructive.

The 118-member High Street Church can neither afford nor justify a full-time resident pastor, much less a part-time director of youth ministries. It is highly unlikely that this congregation will be able to recreate the type and size youth program that Mrs. Barzon enjoyed a generation earlier in a much larger congregation back in that era when relatively few high school students had part-time employment during the academic year.

A more constructive approach might have been to formulate an agenda resembling this one.

1. By definition, the small-membership church is heavily dependent on lay volunteers. Therefore, how do we plan to identify, enlist, train, and support the adult lay volunteers who will staff our youth program?

2. There are six high school students in this congregation. Even if we assume that two or three of them have a friend who would be interested in becoming a part of our youth program, we are talking about a ministry with only seven to ten young people. Therefore, let's not waste our time trying to create a large-group model of a youth program. Let's focus on developing a small-group approach to youth ministries. That means finding at least one adult volunteer who is comfortable and competent in small-group dynamics.

3. For the past several years, this has been an increasingly adult-oriented church. Therefore, if we are to make youth ministries a high priority, we must begin to change the strong adult orientation of this congregation.

4. It is highly unlikely that we will be able to create an effective ministry with youth unless we can develop a consensus on a series of basic questions. Why do we want to have a strong program? For our own children, or to reach beyond our membership? Who wants it? Who are the supportive people and groups who will be active allies in creating a strong youth ministry? What do we hope to accomplish? Do we have widespread support for that goal? What are the priorities among the various hopes and goals people have for the youth program? Can we agree on an approach that will enable us to achieve those goals? What is the role of the young people in determining those goals and priorities?

In addition, we need to look at the criteria for subsequent self-evaluation. Are we looking for large numbers? Or are we primarily concerned about the spiritual and personal growth of our young people? Are we more concerned about a program for children from member families or about reaching teenagers not actively involved in the life of any congregation? Is the number-one objective to teach the Bible? Are we trying to encourage a relationship between each teenager and the church that will continue through adulthood? Do we want to prepare the young people for that eventual move that will take many of them out of their home church and make it easier for them to find a new church home? Are we trying to instill a loyalty to our denominational family? Is our primary goal to help each young person discover what it means to lead a Christian life and to live according to the teachings of Jesus Christ? Are we spending this time, energy, and money in the hope of rearing some replacement leaders and members for our congregation?

While it is tempting to respond "all of the above," that response would be evasive. To plan effectively for youth ministry, a number-one goal is essential.[2] The other "hopes" are secondary or supportive.

5. Some people contend that the single most influential dimension of a congregation's ministry with children and teenagers is to offer them first-hand contacts with a variety of models of *adult* Christians. Perhaps we should see how this can happen here at High Street in several different ways, rather than simply concentrate on an age-segregated youth program. That also may mean we should be looking for mature lay volunteers, rather than a twenty-year-old college student, to staff the program.

6. If we can agree on goals and on an approach to youth ministries, what are the assets, resources, and strengths of this congregation that we can build on in developing that ministry?[3]

While this is not suggested as a universal agenda for this subject, this approach may be more productive than attempting to copy one used by a much larger congregation or attempting to recreate someone else's yesterday.

C. The Financial Base

"I figured it up the other night," announced Glen Erickson, the treasurer of the 93-member Hilltop Church. "We have thirty-seven families or individuals who contributed at least ten dollars last year. Twelve of them accounted for exactly two thirds of our total receipts, and the other twenty-five gave the other third."

"What else is new?" inquired Hank Powers with a touch of sarcasm in his voice. "It's been that way as long as I can remember, and I've been on the Board here, off and on, for nearly forty years."

"Well, it seems to me that if we could get these twenty-five families that give only a third of the total to increase their giving, that would solve our financial problems for a while," replied the treasurer.

This conversation has been repeated thousands of times in hundreds of small congregations. Another version of the same approach to church finances is represented by this statement: "Our budget for next year comes to $42,000. We have two hundred confirmed members. If each one would give four dollars a week, that would cover all our expenses and eliminate our worries."

These comments belong in the same box of diversionary observations as Mrs. Barzon's wish that the 110-member High Street Church could delegate youth ministries to a part-time college student.

A more productive approach might be to begin with this six-point agenda.

1. We know that, in the typical congregation, one third of the people contribute two thirds of the money given by members. Therefore, instead of attempting to persuade everyone to give the same amount, we should review the giving level of that top third. Perhaps our "pacesetters" are setting a very modest pace that inhibits the giving level of the rest of the members.

2. We know our people always support every effort to maintain the church property. Therefore, it might help our financial situation if we had two budgets. One would be for local operating expenses and missions, the second could be a trustees' fund for utilities, insurance, and property maintenance. Some people will give more generously to one budget while others will give more freely to the other. The sum of the two usually will be greater than the total received from member-giving with a single budget.

3. We know we have a number of members who have a very strong interest in missions, while others do not seem to be interested in supporting missions and other denominational causes. Perhaps we should have a separate missions budget and ask people to designate their giving to that cause.

At this point someone may object, "What you're suggesting is doing away with the concept of a unified budget in favor of a far greater emphasis on special appeals! Don't you know that our denominational leadership has been struggling for years to reduce that long list of special offerings in favor of a unified budget?"

When the issue of a unified budget versus special appeals arises, there are at least five issues that must be resolved.

First, the majority of the laity support the case of special, designated, second-mile appeals that provide them with the opportunity to know how their contributions will be used. The higher the level of educational attainment of the contributor, and/or the more "professional" the contributor's vocation, the more likely that lay person will want a voice in how the money will be used.[4]

The laity in congregations with fewer than 150 members are also more likely to believe that knowing how the money will be used influences a person's giving level than is the case with the laity in larger churches.

Second, the unified budget concept has not been adopted as widely by congregations with fewer than 150 members as it has in those congregations with more than 250 members. Money-raising events, special appeals for specific projects, and a less systematic approach to budgeting are characteristics of smaller congregations. Should small-membership churches be expected to adopt and utilize the same administrative systems used in larger congregations?

Third, the unified budget tends to be a loser in an

inflationary era. Special appeals appear to be the more effective means of keeping up with rising costs.

Fourth, a review of the history of the Protestant churches on this continent in the past century suggests very strongly that it is easier to raise money through special, designated, second-mile giving than through a unified budget. Perhaps the most widespread illustration of this point has been the financing of new church buildings. Most of these have been financed by special appeals, rather than through a unified budget. In recent years, the financing of worldwide missions has been heavily dependent on special offerings. The United Presbyterian Church, The American Lutheran Church, the Southern Baptist Convention, The Lutheran Church-Missouri Synod, The Lutheran Church in America, and World Vision, Inc. are among the outstanding practitioners of this concept.

Fifth, and perhaps the most subtle, issue is that the unified budget concept assumes a representative system of church government. That is appropriate for larger congregations. Most small churches, however, operate on something closer to a participatory democracy model of church government. It may be that special offerings are more compatible with the system of church administration followed in smaller congregations, while the unified budget is more appropriate for larger churches. How do your members feel about designated second-mile appeals?

4. Or, if we cannot agree on the possibility of a greater emphasis on special appeals and designated giving, perhaps we should place a greater emphasis on encouraging our members to tithe and to give all or most of that tithe to this church, and/or on a strong emphasis on stewardship? We do know that churches with fewer than 150 members are much less likely than larger congregations to (a) conduct an annual every-member visitation or canvass, (b) place a major emphasis on stewardship, (c) use

stewardship literature, or (d) ask members to make a written financial commitment to that church.[5] Perhaps we need to take a look at how we communicate the financial needs of this parish to our members and at how we ask them to respond.

5. Another option for this agenda is the big one-day appeal, in which an effort is made to raise a huge amount of money for a single cause in one day. In recent years many congregations have had amazing results with this approach. The cause may be an emergency appeal from the denomination, the need to renovate the building, a special mission appeal, the decision to pay off the remaining balance on a high-interest loan, a new organ, or the purchase of a van or church bus, or the construction of a new parsonage. Scores of congregations have raised an amount equal to somewhere between one third of the total annual budget and twice the annual budget in these appeals, which raise a huge amount of cash in a very brief period of time. It is essential that the cause be attractive, that there be a broad base of congregational cause, and that the special appeal be preceded by an adequate informational effort.

6. Or, if no one is satisfied with any of these alternatives, perhaps we should seek some outside assistance. Would it be helpful to bring someone in to conduct a stewardship workshop to help our members understand that we are not asking them to give simply to underwrite our church expenses, but to give out of a sense of gratitude to God for all he has given to us?

Would any of these six agenda items fit your congregation as you talk about strengthening the financial base for ministry? As you reflect on these and other alternative courses of action, please keep in mind the central thesis of this book. The small-membership church is different. Therefore, be cautious about any suggestion to force a large-church procedure or technique on the small congregation.

D. Church Growth

"There must be at least two dozen families who have moved into this community in the past couple of years," observed Ben Whitaker, "but the only ones who have come to this church are Ed and Barbara Campbell. New people are moving in; how come we're not growing?"

"You have to remember that Barbara grew up in this church, and that's why the Campbells came here. Her folks are both dead now, but she still has several friends here from when she was here as a child," added Irene Hawkins. "I really can't understand, however, why we're not getting some of the other new families moving here."

"Well, the doors are open," commented Martha Williams, rather tartly. "If they're interested in coming to church, all they have to do is to walk in. The Lord only knows we need more people to help pay the bills. If we don't start getting some new blood pretty soon, this church is going to die."

"I guess we have a generation coming along that's just not interested in organized religion," remarked Herb Addison, a long-time member of this 168-member congregation. "When we moved here back right after World War II, it seems that nearly everyone went to church. Now a lot of the younger folks have too many other things to do on the weekends, and I guess they don't have time for church."

"Well, I sure hate to see our church getting smaller when there are people moving in here who aren't going to any church," continued Ben Whitaker. "I wish there was some way we could attract them to come here."

One approach to the issue of church growth and decline is to speculate on what people who are not coming to our church are thinking or doing. Another approach is to assume that the enlistment of new members is the responsibility of the minister.

A more constructive approach might be to develop a strategy for new-member recruitment. Here again, it is important to tailor that strategy to the resources and distinctive characteristics of the small church rather than to attempt to copy a large-church model. The process for developing this strategy in many small congregations probably should include consideration of these twelve questions.

1. What is the level of congregational self-esteem here? How do our members view this church? Do they "poor mouth" it when talking with their friends? Or do our members have a healthy pride in this congregation? In most numerically growing churches the members are enthusiastic about (a) their faith as Christians, (b) the congregation of which they are members, and (c) their minister. (Two out of three does *not* yield a passing grade!) If the members of your church do not have a strong, positive self-image, rectifying that should be the first step in developing a church growth strategy.

2. What is the time frame used for planning and program development? As was pointed out in the previous chapter, a common characteristic of small-membership churches is they often use a short time frame for planning. Most growing churches have found it necessary to follow a two to three-year time frame in order to develop an effective evangelistic outreach to unchurched persons. This is essential if the strategy places a heavy reliance on either newspaper advertising or on direct-mail evangelism.

Perhaps the simplest beginning point for lengthening that time frame is to secure a few copies of a three-year calendar. One should be posted where members gather to socialize, one in the minister's office, one on the wall where the governing board meets, and perhaps one in the room where that adult Sunday school class, which has so much influence, meets. (In some buildings this will require only two copies of the calendar.)

The second step is to begin to plan and schedule events and programs that will reinforce the evangelistic outreach of this congregation, and to note them on the calendar. These might include an extensive newspaper advertising campaign, a lay witness weekend, a workshop on church growth, a training program to equip members for a visitation-evangelism program, a direct-mail evangelism effort, a revival, a series of special programs designed to meet the needs of one segment of the unchurched population in that community, the launching of a new Sunday school class designed to reach beyond the membership, or some other church growth emphasis. It is much easier to schedule these before the calendar is filled up with the traditional local programs and events. More important, once the church growth events have been scheduled and are on those highly visible calendars, this will allow adequate time for planning, stimulate members' creativity, and help reinforce the concept that church growth is a priority here.

3. What is the average tenure of our ministers? Congregations that have experienced a long series of two or three-year pastorates tend to be either numerically declining churches or on a plateau in size. That is a statement of fact that can be documented in nearly every denominational family in the second half of the twentieth century.

While there is absolutely no evidence to prove that long pastorates automatically produce numerically growing congregations, it is rare to find a small congregation that has experienced substantial numerical growth, *and sustained that growth*, without the benefit of a long pastorate. (The two major exceptions to that generalization are new missions less than three or four years old and congregations with an extensive organization of lay-managed face-to-face groups, such as the traditional adult Sunday school.)

Therefore, it may be that one of the components for an effective church growth strategy in your congregation would be to encourage longer pastorates. Among the means of doing this are (a) a strong affirmation of the pastor's ministry, (b) housing appropriate to that minister's needs, (c) strong affirmation of the pastor's spouse, (d) enhancing the opportunities for the pastor to gain a feeling of satisfaction from his or her ministry, (e) better economic compensation, and (f) perhaps most important of all, a mutual commitment to a three to five-year plan of ministry.

4. What are the priorities we place on the minister's time and energy? That word "we" includes *both* the laity and the minister! What proportion of the minister's time and energy is spent on the members and on congregational concerns? What proportion is spent with non-members and with prospective members? What proportion is spent on developing and implementing a new-member recruitment strategy?

In most small-membership churches (and in nearly all very large congregations) the minister is a key factor in any strategy for new-member enlistment. In addition to long tenure, this usually means that a large proportion of the minister's time and energy must be reserved for face-to-face contacts with potential new members and new members. Obviously that reduces the amount of time the minister has to spend with members. This is one of the basic prices of church growth, and one that many members are unwilling to pay.

In the thousands of small congregations that share one minister's time and energy with one or more other congregations, this often means the pastor must be willing and free to carry on a "maintenance level" ministry in one or two congregations and budget his or her discretionary time very carefully in order to participate in a church growth strategy with one congregation in the multi-church parish.

Frequently the minister is the central figure in the small church's new-member recruitment strategy. It is very, very difficult for one minister to be the central figure in a church growth plan in two different congregations at the same time! That is another price that many people are unwilling to pay.

If your congregation is part of a multi-church parish, in which congregation will the minister be free to focus on church growth? Who decided that? Is there widespread agreement on it?

5. What are the strengths, resources and assets? Too many small-membership churches spend an excessive amount of time lamenting their weaknesses, bemoaning their shortcomings, and emphasizing their limitations. A more productive approach is to identify, affirm, and plan to build on strengths. There is a significant number of unchurched persons, for example, who would find the friendliness, the ability of most members to call everyone by name, the spontaneity, the caring, the fellowship, the intimacy, and the warmth of the small church to be what they seek in a church, but all of their previous experiences with churches have caused them to believe this does not exist anywhere today.

Some small congregations have several widowed members who can be the central resource in developing a very redemptive ministry to the recently widowed. Others have a strong intergenerational character that can be an asset in reaching some people living in one or two-generation households.

What are the assets in your congregation that could be

foundation stones for expanding the evangelistic outreach of your congregation?

6. Who are the people in this general community who are largely overlooked by the churches? What are their needs? Which of these needs could we respond to if we decided to make the effort?

While it rarely will be the first question that should be raised in developing church growth strategy in the small congregation, this is the pivotal question. There are at least three reasons why it is *the* central question.

First, this question will help focus the members' attention on the unmet needs of people outside the worshiping congregation. That is the key factor in developing an effective evangelistic outreach. Too often, small-membership churches begin their planning because "we need some new members or our church may close."

Second, this question supplements the previous question on resources and assets. The most effective new-member recruitment strategies utilize the strengths of the congregation as the foundation for responding to people's unmet needs.

Third, any thorough effort to identify the unmet needs of people who are largely overlooked by most churches will produce a long list of needs. The sheer length of this list often will force the leaders in the small-membership church to limit their responses to those needs for which they have, or can mobilize, the appropriate resources, and to begin to develop the concept of a clearly defined "target group." No one congregation is able to respond effectively to the needs of everyone. Every congregation reaches and serves only a small slice of the total spectrum of the population.[6] Thus this question on the needs of the unchurched tends to encourage leaders to focus on the needs that match their resources, rather than to sit back and wish "that everyone would come join our wonderful fellowship here."

POTENTIAL NEW GROUPS

Fishermen's Club
Mothers of Twins
New Roots (troubled
  wives of husbands
  who have been
  transferred)
Bethel
People Who Work
  Nights
C Section
Prayer Group
Ex-Homemakers
Junior Choir
Parenting
Harvesters Club
Alanon
S. S. Teachers
Volleyball
Chrismons
Crafts
Nursing Home Callers
Band Mothers
Men's Club
Orchestra
Quarterly Clean Up
Cabin in the Woods
Adult Choir
Banner Group
Quilting
New Mothers
Stepmothers
Visit Another Similar
  Church

New Members
Senior Citizens
Recently Divorced
Empty Nesters
Newlyweds
Sew for Others
Recently Widowed
Fun Choir
Co-ed Circle (in the
    Women's Organiza-
    tion)
Breakaway (for
    empty nest mothers
    ready to break away
    from old routines)
Travel Club
Garden Club
Softball Team
Young Singles
Parents Who Recently
  Experienced the
  Death of a Child
Camera Club
Ex-Iowans
Men and Boys' Chorus
Altar Guild
Single Parents
Drama Group
Newly Retired
Brass Ensemble
Parents of Teenagers
Handbell Choir
Bowling League

7. What new ministries, programs, groups, circles, or organizations must we consider if we are to reach, attract and assimilate more people? This may be the second most important question in this process of developing a church growth strategy. There are at least ten reasons why this is an important question.

First, the creation of new face-to-face groups is a widely used, and usually very effective, response to unmet needs.

Second, it is an operational response to the generalization, "create new groups to reach and assimilate new people."

Third, it is an operational means of challenging people's creativity.

Fourth, most small-membership churches tend to be perceived by outsiders as exclusionary. The creation of new face-to-face groups creates new and comparatively open entry points for some of these people.

Fifth, it follows one of the basic principles of planned change by addition, not by subtraction or division.

Sixth, it creates new opportunities for newcomers to feel needed, wanted and valued. (You know you belong when you know you are needed.)

Seventh, it reduces the risk of alienating some of the oldtimers, since existing groups are not challenged or changed.

Eighth, it creates a need for new talents, skills, gifts, and expressions of commitment.

Ninth, it opens a door for newcomers who have been attracted by the magnetic personality of the pastor, to begin to develop a meaningful relationship with the congregation.

Tenth, it is an operational expression of one of the most effective approaches to leadership: leaders come through organization. The stronger and the more extensive the organizational structure, the easier it is to discover and develop new leadership. This principle applies to churches of all sizes.

8. Who are the allies in implementing this strategy? There is not an easy-to-define best time for asking this question, but it is a question that the chief architects of a church growth strategy must ask. Sometimes it may be better to wait until it is possible to define a precisely stated responsibility with a clearly stated terminal date, before certain members are asked to join the alliance. It is easier to enlist volunteers when the task is stated in very precise terms.

9. What proportion of our budget is allocated to financing the costs of implementing a church growth strategy? Sooner or later the question of money will arise. The congregation that is seriously interested in an effective church growth strategy should expect to allocate three to eight percent of the total church budget for such items as postage, printing, newspaper advertising,[7] radio spots, training programs for lay leadership, signs, posters, continuing education experiences, resources for creating new groups, and other components of the strategy.

What percentage of your church budget is allocated for the implementation of a church growth strategy?

10. How restrictive are we on the use of our building? Many congregations have charged the trustees with the responsibility to maintain the building in a like-new condition. One of the ways of accomplishing this is to minimize the use of the building. What are the official, and unofficial, restrictions on the use of your building? Which of these may have to be changed in order to implement a church growth strategy? Who will take the lead in accomplishing these changes in policy?

11. What changes in the schedule, in the organizational structure, and in the priorities of this congregation will have

to be made in order to implement our church growth strategy?

These might include changes in the Sunday morning schedule, in the priorities in the allocation of financial resources, in the assignment of space in the building for program activities, in the sharing of the minister's time, in the lifting up of the importance of certain program committees, or in the worship experience.

What changes will you have to make in your congregation to facilitate numerical growth?

12. What are the priorities in nominating lay volunteers for leadership and worker responsibilities? In some small-membership churches, the most competent and influential lay volunteers are "creamed off" to serve as trustees, on the finance committee, or on the board. In other churches the most talented and committed lay volunteers are asked to serve on the evangelism committee, act as greeters, be Sunday school teachers, and make visitation-evangelism calls. What are the priorities in your church?

Now, how many of these questions should be on the agenda as you develop and implement a strategy for church growth in your congregation?

Finally, there is a unique dimension to church growth in the small congregation that frequently is overlooked. This is the impact of newcomers on the ongoing life of the small church.

The typical thousand-member congregation must receive an average of 60 to 125 members annually in order to remain on a plateau in size. This is an average of one or two a week. This means the congregation becomes accustomed to an average of four to eight strangers coming into that congregation every month. Very few members of the larger churches feel an obligation to make friends with every one of the new members. Frequently, however, some of the new members and many of the long-time members become acquainted on a first-name basis.

Furthermore, many of the members in the larger churches have spent many years as a part of a subgroup, class, or a social group that has a modest degree of turnover in the membership. New groups are created to absorb many of the adult newcomers.

These patterns mean that, in the larger churches, new members can be received in rather large numbers without the process' becoming disruptive.

By contrast, the typical small-membership churches receive an average of only four to ten new members a year, and perhaps one-half or more of those come in via family ties. Some of these new members are children of members who were reared in that congregation, and one or two may be people who married members. Thus the statistical report that shows seven new members received last year may include only one or two people who do not have kinfolk ties to the congregation. This is not comparable to the thousand-member church that may receive forty to sixty strangers as members every year.

What are the implications of this difference?

First, it means the larger churches often have extensive experience in assimilating new strangers into the membership, but many small congregations have had little practice with the process.

Second, in the larger congregations, adult new members frequently are first assimilated into face-to-face groups where they feel wanted, needed, appreciated, and welcomed. The creation of new groups to absorb new members means the influx of strangers has few, if any, negative effects on either the ongoing life of the congregation as a whole, or on those long-established and tightly knit groups in which four-fifths of the members have been part of the group or class for several years.

The Small Church Is Different!

By contrast, the single-cell small church often functions as one large group. New members either are absorbed into that central fellowship or feel left out. Frequently, that single fellowship cell is already as large as it can become without changing the character and quality of the interpersonal relationships. Replacements can be absorbed, but it cannot grow in size without serious internal stress. In other words, large churches can often absorb fifty or sixty strangers annually without any disruption, but the typical small church will have difficulty in absorbing more than two or three strangers each year.

Third, this helps explain why those congregations (regardless of size) that have a strong network of face-to-face groups find it relatively easy to reach and assimilate strangers, but single-cell congregations (again regardless of size), tend to remain on a plateau in size or to show a gradual decline.

Fourth, this concept also helps to explain "the alienation of the oldtimers" that often occurs when small-membership churches do reach, attract, and assimilate ten or twenty new adults annually and perhaps double in size in four or more years.

If newcomers are assimilated largely through the process of creating new face-to-face groups, some of the oldtimers may feel alienated. The whole picture of congregational life has expanded so swiftly that they find it harder to comprehend the entire scene. Some feel overwhelmed.

Sometimes a "no win" situation is created. If new groups are started to help assimilate the new members, some of the members of the long-established groups and classes may feel, "That's not right! We need some new blood and some fresh faces to keep our group going." If the new members are successfully directed into the long-established groups, some of the oldtimers may feel, "These new people have taken over our class and have made so many changes that I don't know what's going on any more, so I'll just stay home and let them run it."

If, on the other hand, a successful effort is made to assimilate the newcomers into that central fellowship circle, some of the oldtimers, who would keep up with what was going on in a group of ten, fifteen, or twenty people, have difficulty staying near the center of a group of forty or fifty. They feel they are drifting to the outer edge of the group, and they begin to feel left out. Some begin to drop out and are hurt when they discover no one missed them. The feeling of alienation deepens. The alienation is reinforced when some of their long-time friends rejoice in the growth, in the opportunity to meet and make new friends, and in the excitement that has accompanied the increase in the size and activity of what once was a small church. The alienated oldtimer now begins to feel more neglected. "In the old days Helen used to stop by to see me at least three or four times a week. Now she's so busy with all of her new friends that she's forgotten all about me."

Fifth, in the thousand-member church, which usually is understaffed, the pastor often has a very limited amount of time to spend visiting members. By contrast, in thousands of small-membership churches, a regular visit from the minister is a part of the expectations of many members. In fact, that is why some people prefer a small congregation. They have the opportunity for greater personal contact with the minister.

Thus when the pastor of the large church spends a fair amount of time every month with prospective new members and new members, most of the members do not feel rejected. They weren't accustomed to regular visits from the minister.

By contrast, however, when the minister of the small-membership church spends considerable time in the first year or two of a new pastorate visiting with the members, "getting acquainted and building the trust level," a pattern of expectations has been established. Later on, in year two or three of that pastorate, when the minister begins to spend more time with prospective new members, on expanding the program in order to assimilate the new-comers, and in visiting with new members, some of the oldtimers may begin to feel neglected. "I wonder if he remembers who is paying his salary?" "Sometimes I think she forgets that I was one of those who voted to call a woman pastor." "How long has it been since the new minister stopped by to see you?"

Finally, if the thousand-member congregation receives a total of four hundred new members in a three-year period for a net increase of two hundred, that usually does not require the long-time members to adjust to many changes. There are some new faces in what is now a larger choir, one or two new circles have been added to the women's organization, a few of the leaders and several of the Sunday school teachers are new; but overall, not much appears to have changed. Basically, it's more of the same.

By contrast, however, if the congregation that has been averaging 45 at worship on Sunday morning for many years shows a net increase of ten per year at worship for three consecutive years, it may mean many changes. The church now has a choir every Sunday, half of the board members are new, one third of the people at worship were complete strangers three years earlier, the member who always prided herself on being able to call everyone by name may now have difficulty remembering which children belong to which parents, sometimes a new member sits in a pew that was always reserved for Mr. and Mrs. Rogers, there is now some discontent if the worship service does not begin and end right on time, a couple of the new members have been embarrassed when they said the wrong thing to the wrong person because the new member was not aware of the kinfolk ties, and there has been a sharp expansion of the whole program.

A net gain of a hundred or two does not make much difference in the big church, but a new increase of twenty or thirty or forty can radically alter the flow and style of congregational life in the small church.

Therefore, a church growth agenda in the small-membership church may be enriched by asking these five questions.

1. If we are successful in attracting new members, what can we do to help *all* of the long-time members feel some sense of "ownership" of that effort? (Ownership reduces alienation.)

2. If we do attract more new members, how can we help the new members and the oldtimers become better acquainted?

3. If our church does grow in numbers, should we start a weekly or monthly parish newsletter?

4. If our church does grow, how do we go about introducing new ideas in programming, changes in schedules, and new goals in a manner that will maximize support and minimize alienation?

5. What can we do to help the members accept the fact that church growth means a major change in the priorities on the minister's time and energy?

It also must be recognized that, if the small church that has been averaging 25 to 50 at worship for many years grows to a point that it is now averaging 60 to 80 at worship, this will also have serious implications for staffing—but that's a whole new subject and deserves a new chapter.

Chapter III

STAFFING
THE SMALL CHURCH

Do you realize the consumer price index tripled between 1965 and 1983, but our budget for this year is only a little over double what it was back in 1965? Do you know what it costs for pension, health insurance, car allowance, continuing education, and other items that a congregation is expected to include in the compensation for a pastor?" asked the irate treasurer of the 188-member Emmanuel Church. "Do you know how much of our total budget goes to the minister? I'll tell you. Just a shade less than 60 percent of our budget goes to the minister! That includes his cash salary, housing allowance, reimbursement for mileage, pension, health insurance, and the $300 we allow for continuing education and conference expenses. Back in 1963 when I took this job as church treasurer, 42 percent of our budget went to the minister. Now it's 59 percent, and I expect next year it will be over 60 percent. How does anyone expect a church like ours to be able to keep the doors open?"

The comments of this church treasurer illustrate four trends that are very significant to anyone concerned about providing ministerial leadership for small-membership churches.

First, and most important, the inflationary wave that traces back to the mid-nineteen-sixties simply has priced many churches out of the ministerial marketplace. One evidence of this trend is the large congregation that had three full-time ordained ministers on the staff in 1967, and now has only two. Another is the decline in the number of clergy in the pastoral ministry in several denominations. Perhaps more serious in some respects is the decreasing number of members per ordained minister, or per 1,000 ministers serving congregations as pastors or associate ministers. When there was an average of 300 or more members for each ordained minister, the financial load on the congregation was less than when that ratio dropped to 250 members for each minister.[1]

The second trend illustrated by this treasurer's comments reflects the impact of inflation. During an eighteen-year period of time, the consumer price index tripled, the average ministerial salary increased about two and a half times, but the receipts from members giving only doubled. Eventually that squeeze must show up in other parts of the budget.

A third trend is the proportion of the total receipts allocated to the combined costs of maintaining a minister. Several denominational officials have used the rule of thumb that when that percentage exceeds 40 percent of all expenditures, that raises a warning signal. In general, whenever a congregation allocates more than 40 percent of the total budget for ministerial compensation (including cash salary, housing costs, pension,* health insurance,* travel costs, continuing education,* and conference expenses*) that often means that program costs, missions, and/or building maintenance are underfinanced. Whenever that proportion passes the 50 percent figure, it almost always means other needs and causes are underfinanced.

A fourth trend that is reflected in the comments of the Emmanuel Church treasurer can be summarized by this question. "What is the smallest size congregation that can

---

*In some denominations, with The United Methodist Church being the outstanding example, this is not easy to calculate; since many of these costs are included in apportionments and may add up to $6,000 to $8,000 per year for each minister on the staff.

command the services of a full-time ordained minister and still be a viable unit in terms of program, outreach, and mission?"

During the depths of the Great Depression in the early 1930s, it was not difficult to find a congregation in a small town that averaged thirty to forty people at worship on Sunday morning, was served by a full-time married minister whose wife was not employed outside the home, and the minister did not have any outside source of income except for the garden in the back yard.

Twenty years later, that average attendance figure had to be raised to fifty to sixty to enable one to find many churches with a full-time ordained minister—and there was approximately one chance in four that the minister's wife was employed outside the home.

If that survey was conducted in the mid-1970s, average attendance had to be raised to between 70 to 80 to include a substantial number of congregations with their own pastors—and there was slightly over a fifty-fifty chance that the pastor's spouse was employed outside the home, and a fair chance the minister either had part-time employment or was in school.

By the early 1980s that average worship attendance was up to 120 to 140 in several denominations* and there was an

---

*There are four major exceptions to the current figures on the minimum size to be a viable congregation with a full-time resident minister. First, in the West and in the mid-South there are hundreds of congregations averaging 40 to 80 at worship with their own full-time resident pastor. Second, several denominations now provide direct or indirect subsidies to small churches to enable them to continue with a full-time minister, although that is a diminishing trend. Third, the sharp increase in the number of clergy couples has enabled many congregations to secure the services of a full-time minister, even though that congregation's worship attendance may be in the 40 to 75 range. Finally, in several smaller denominations in which the members have a high degree of congregational and denominational loyalty, tithing is a much more common

even greater possibility that the minister's spouse was employed outside the home. This sharp increase in the minimum size of the congregations that are able to secure the services of a full-time resident minister must be examined in a larger context before moving on to a discussion of alternative courses of action in staffing small-membership churches.

A. What Is the Context?

The most obvious part of the context for looking at the implications of this trend can be found in the chart on page 58. One half of the Protestant congregations in the United States and Canada have fewer than 75 people at worship on the typical Sunday morning. Does that mean that one half of all churches are not viable units?

Of course not! The ability to support a full-time minister has nothing to do with the viability of a worshiping congregation! If one looks at the history of the Christian churches through the centuries, it quickly becomes apparent that some of the most redemptive, influential, faithful, obedient, and effective worshiping congregations did not have the services of a "set apart" paid minister who had no other source of income except that congregation.

What this does mean is that perhaps one half to two thirds of all Protestant congregations on the North American continent must look at some other alternatives. This is *not* news. Only one third of all United Methodist congregations in the United States, for example, are served by a minister who does not serve any other church, who is not in school and who does not have any other employment. More than

---

practice, and ministerial salaries are below average, it is still not uncommon to find a congregation averaging fifty to seventy-five people at the principal worship service with a full-time resident minister, but with no denominational subsidy and a good level of mission giving.

one fourth of all Southern Baptist ministers are bivocational and are involved in a secular job while serving a church. One out of six Episcopal priests serving parishes also has part-time or full-time employment outside the parish.

What this suggests is that the traditional dream of "having our own pastor" who does not have any outside demands on his or her time is not a realistic goal for at least half of all the Protestant churches on the North American continent.

A second part of the context for looking at this issue is a phenomenon that touches all segments of life. The cost of providing person-centered services has been rising much faster than the increase in people's income.[2] The average hospital charge per patient day rose from $5.21 in 1946, to $8 in 1950, to $16 in 1960, to $54 in 1970, to nearly $300 in 1983. Between 1960 and 1980 the number of students enrolled in public schools (grades 1-12) increased from 36.5 million to 43 million, but expenditures increased from $19 billion in 1960 to $95 billion in 1980, or from $520 per student to $2210 per student. The cost of providing professional services to people has been going up very rapidly for more than thirty years. The cost of providing ministerial services to church members has not been completely immune to this trend. When compared to the level of living of the rest of the population, a congregation of 250 members was necessary in 1980 to provide a pastor compensation equivalent to that offered by the congregation of 85 members in 1935.

A third part of the context for looking at the squeeze on the small churches and at alternatives in staffing is the tremendous increase in the number of ordained ministers. In the Presbyterian Church in the United States, for example, there were 3,438 churches in 1915 and 4,067 in 1979, but the number of ordained ministers rose from 1,850 in 1915, to 3,733 in 1960, to 5,431 in 1979—an increase from an average of 0.5 ministers per congregation in 1915 to 1.33 ministers per congregation in 1979. In the United Presbyterian Church in the U.S.A. the number of clergy rose from 9,473 in 1951 to 13,846 in 1976. Similar trends have prevailed in many other denominations. In simple terms, there are thousands of seminary-trained ministers out there who might be interested in something other than the traditional arrangement for providing churches with pastoral leadership.

Fourth, there is the rapid increase in the number of two-career married couples. Some of these two-career marriages include a seminary-trained spouse who (a) seeks either full-time or part-time employment as a pastor, (b) places the value of living with his or her spouse above the value of flexibility in choosing a church, and (c) may be open to some nontraditional arrangements in serving as the pastor of a worshiping congregation.

Finally, the last half of the twentieth century brought a surge of interest in several overlapping concepts. These included (a) the nonstipendiary clergy, (b) the worker-priest, (c) the tentmaker-pastor, (d) dual-role clergy, (e) bivocational ministers, and similar concepts. In each case the concept called for the minister to be gainfully employed outside the parish in addition to continuing to serve in a ministerial role.

Now, before reviewing alternative approaches, it may help to examine three widely neglected criteria for evaluating these alternatives.

B. Three Neglected Criteria

One of the most widely shared values among church members is that every congregation should have its own full-time* resident pastor who does not have any other employment and does not serve any other congregation.

---

*In several parts of the United States, the term "full-time" does *not* mean the minister is a full-time employee of that congregation without any other

The Small Church Is Different!

Church members especially like to have the complete attention of their pastor on the Sabbath. Given a choice between a minister who holds a 20 to 40-hour-a-week secular job or is in school and serves that congregation on a part-time basis; *or* a minister who has no secular employment, but divides his or her time among two or more congregations, most members would choose the first arrangement. They would prefer to share their minister with a secular employer rather than with another congregation.

This is not a surprising response, but one that is not widely appreciated. There appear to be many reasons for this preference. One is the obvious fact that the minister with a secular job usually is available for the full day and evening on Sunday, while the minister serving a two- or three-church parish has limited availability in each church on the Sabbath. Another is based on the assumption that Carl Dudley is correct when he asserts that the small church wants its minister to be a "lover."[3] That may be the most meaningful term to use in describing the key role of the pastor of the small church; and if it is, the second church in a two-church parish may be perceived as a rival for our lover's affections. By contrast, the secular employer who demands part of our lover's time will usually be seen in functional, economic, and professional terms, rather than as a threat. The rivalry is over time, not over affections. A third reason for this preference may be that the conflicts over time with a secular employer usually focus on the relatively unimportant hours of Monday through Friday, while the conflicts over time with another

employment. It means that congregation has the only claim on the minister's pastoral services. That minister does not serve any other congregation, but may hold a secular job. It also should be noted that in scores of churches in the rural South, "full-time" has nothing to do with the role of the minister. A "full-time church" is one that has a preaching service *every* Sunday morning and every Sunday evening.

congregation in a two-church parish tend to be focused on those very important hours of the Sabbath.

This distinction between sharing the affections of our lover with another church and sharing the time of our minister with another employer is one of the most widely neglected criteria in evaluating alternative means of staffing small congregations.

A second yardstick for evaluating alternatives in providing small churches with ministerial leadership overlaps this first one. What are the most productive minutes in the week? For many ministers, the minutes before the Sunday morning worship service, during that fellowship period between the Sunday school hour and the worship hour, and while people are preparing to leave the building, can be the most productive minutes in the week for pastoral care. More can be done in less time than on any other day of the week. Thus a second criterion for evaluation should be how to maximize those productive minutes.

The third guideline that also tends to be overlooked concerns the importance of continuity. Alvin Toffler was correct in his declaration that people need "stability zones."[4] One dimension of stability is continuity. Another is predictability. If one accepts the basic assumption made earlier that every change in ministers tends to be a disruptive event, it may be wise not to subject the small church to an excessive number of disruptions. Therefore, a third criterion should be how to lengthen the tenure of the minister serving the small-membership church. One of the means of lengthening the tenure for the minister is to choose an alternative that is likely to provide many satisfactions for the pastor.

C. What Are the Alternatives?

The past four decades have brought an unparalleled variety of changes to the social and economic structure in which the small church functions. One of these, which was referred to earlier, is the longest inflationary cycle in American history. That has reduced the proportion of Protestant churches that can afford to have their own full-time resident minister. Most of the changes of the past forty years, however, have resulted in a sharp expansion in the range of choices open to the leaders of small churches as they seek ministerial leadership. This point can be made most effectively by reviewing a dozen of these alternatives.

1. *The full-time pastor*

While many congregations have been priced out of the possibility of having their own full-time minister, this is the first preference of most members and therefore it belongs at the top of this list of alternatives. It is still available to many small-membership churches, including (1) the congregation with twelve to twenty families in which every family tithes and gives that entire tithe to the church, (2) the congregation with a substantial endowment fund, (3) the small-membership church that is financially subsidized by the denomination because of a distinctive witness and/or the potential for growth, (4) the congregation served by one member of a clergy couple who does not need or seek full-time compensation including housing, (5) the congregation served by an older minister who has technically retired, and therefore receives less than minimum salary but continues to work on a full-time basis, (6) the congregation served by the retired military chaplain who chooses that community as a place of future retirement, but is still interested in full-time service, (7) the ordained member of a two-career couple who has chosen to live here because it was the lay spouse's turn to pick "where we live next," and who is available to serve this small church, but does not need housing and/or a full-time salary, (8) the congregation at the larger end of the size bracket labeled "small-membership churches"—typically those averaging 60 to 100 at worship on Sunday morning—that can pay the salary of a full-time resident pastor by the combination of generous giving and careful budgeting, but does not want either direct or indirect financial subsidies from the denomination, (9) the congregation served by the full-time minister who went into the professional ministry as a second career late in life and who does not need full-time compensation, (10) the small, but wealthy congregation that seeks and can afford a full-time minister for a small number of members, (11) the congregation served by the single minister who does not want or need the compensation package required by the married minister who is rearing a family, (12) the congregation served by the person who left the ministry and now seeks to reenter the pastoral ministry and accepts the fact this may mean reentering via a small congregation with a subminimum compensation package, (13) the ordained denominational staff person who took early retirement and is now finishing out a ministerial career in a small, stable congregation, and (14) the minister who, for health reasons, has had to move from a high-stress pastorate, but who wants to continue as a pastor on a full-time basis, but does not need minimum salary.

While that list of exceptions is not complete, it is long enough to suggest that the option of "our own full-time pastor" is a realistic possibility for thousands and thousands of small-membership churches.

2. The bivocational pastor

The fastest growing alternative on this list is the dual-role or bivocational minister.[5] In this arrangement, the minister contracts with a congregation for approximately twenty hours of ministerial services a week. The larger source of income for that minister, however, is a secular job that usually requires 32 to 45 hours a week.

The Southern Baptist Convention has developed a major program thrust to encourage small-membership churches to consider this alternative. Approximately 29 percent of all ministers in the Southern Baptist Convention now serve in a bivocational role.

This is not a new concept! Paul was a tentmaker. During the nineteenth century and the first third of the twentieth century, tens of thousands of Baptist, Nazarene, Holiness, Methodist, Christian, and Presbyterian preachers gained most of their economic compensation from secular employment. Most of these ministers were not college graduates and many had not graduated from high school. The majority were farmers, in the building trades, or semi-skilled laborers.

Today's roster of bivocational ministers includes seminary professors, school teachers, forest rangers, salespersons, carpenters, mail carriers, attorneys, social workers, military personnel, engineers, insurance agents, farmers, college professors, physicians, accountants, and literally scores of other vocations.

Today a growing proportion of bivocational ministers have graduated from an accredited theological seminary, have been ordained and carry full ministerial standing in their denomination, and have served as full-time pastors. A few are now serving, on a part-time basis, the same congregation they had served earlier on a full-time schedule.

Many, perhaps even a majority, of bivocational pastors live in one community, work in a second, and serve a church located in a third community. This facilitates a clarity of role definition. Each role is the only role that minister fills in that particular environment and with the people in that community.

The CODE project in upper New York State found that twenty to twenty-five hours a week was the recommended minimum involvement in the ministry of the church if it was to be more than a maintenance program for the congregation. Certain legal and pension benefits also are available only to ministers who invest twenty or more hours a week in their pastoral duties.

Among the advantages of this approach to staffiing churches with ministerial leadership are (a) it provides many satisfactions for the pastor who otherwise might be underemployed as the full-time minister of a small congregation, (b) it has enabled many small churches to have the ministerial services of a pastor who is not diverted at peak hour times by serving one or more other congregations, (c) it strengthens the role of the laity in ministry, (d) it enables small-membership congregations to concentrate a larger proportion of their resources on mission and ministry, rather than being excessively concerned with raising money to support a minister (remember the comments of the church treasurer in the opening paragraph of this chapter), (e) it tends to produce longer pastorates with the benefits that accompany that pattern, (f) it clarifies the distinction between what the professional minister should do, and what can be done, often better, by lay volunteers, (g) it usually eliminates the need for a financial subsidy from the denomination with all the benefits that go with that new freedom from dependency, (h) it reduces the minister's sense of dependency on the congregation, (i) it means a smaller proportion of the church budget is allocated to ministerial compensation, (j) the secular job enables the minister to gain a new perspective on the life and pressures on the lay volunteer in the church, and (k) it is a response to the surplus in the number of seminary-trained ministers in several denominations.

The three major shortcomings of this approach that are cited most often are that (a) it requires the minister to be able and willing to work fifty-five to sixty-five hours a week, which requires a capability to manage one's time very effectively—a capability not possessed by every minister, (b) in the clergy-dominated denominations, such as The United Methodist Church, in which the minister, rather than the laity, is the critical link between the congregation and the denomination, this may weaken the denominational tie, and (c) the pastor often is not able to attend daytime denominational or ministerial meetings scheduled during the week.

The concept of bivocational or dual-career minister probably will be one of the more rapidly growing movements during the 1980s in the United Presbyterian Church, The United Methodist Church, the Lutheran Church in America, the Cumberland Presbyterian Church, The United Church of Christ, The American Baptist Churches, and The Christian Church (Disciples of Christ); as well as in those denominational families in which it already is firmly established, such as Episcopalians, Mennonites, Brethren, Nazarenes, and thousands of black and Hispanic congregations.

3. *The multi-church parish or the circuit*

While support for this alternative has been diminishing in recent years, thousands of smaller congregations share a pastor with one or more congregations from the same denominational family. The United Methodist Church and the Lutheran Church in America have been the leaders in the practice of this arrangement, although it is widely used by at least a dozen other denominations, including the

Lutheran Church-Missouri Synod, the United Presbyterian Church, and The United Church of Christ.

In the typical arrangement, the minister serves on a full-time basis, has no outside employment, the economic compensation package is divided among the participating congregations, and the minister preaches at two or three different places every Sunday morning. Sometimes a lay volunteer serves as liturgist and begins the worship service at the second (or third) church on the Sunday morning schedule, in case the preacher's arrival has been delayed.

Frequently the only things the participating churches have in common are (a) they are part of the same denomination, (b) they share the minister's time, (c) they divide the cost of the minister's compensation among them, and (d) they may have a joint personnel, search, or pastor-parish relations committee that is responsible for seeking a new minister when the present pastor departs. Occasionally they do some joint programming together, such as a Good Friday service, a Thanksgiving service, or a youth group, but that is not the usual pattern.

The scale of this approach can be seen by the fact that in The United Methodist Church, more than 17,000 churches out of the 38,500 congregations in the denomination, share a pastor with one or two other congregations; and another 5,500 congregations are linked together in an arrangement in which one minister serves four or more congregations. The concept of a full-time resident minister who is not in school, does not serve any other church, and does not have any secular employment describes slightly less than one third of all United Methodist churches in the United States.

The advantages of this system include: (a) the fact that usually, but not always, the pastor has a full-time commitment to the parish ministry, (b) the cost of the minister's compensation is shared by several congregations, (c) the minister has the challenge of a full-time workload, (d) the minister is readily available for both congregational and denominational needs during the week, (e) the young minister coming directly from seminary gains experience with two or three different (and sometimes very different) congregations in a brief period of time, (f) it may reinforce the identification with the denomination, and (g) sometimes it is a very efficient system for providing a ministry to people in nursing homes and hospitals, since one minister can call on people from two or three congregations in one trip, and each receives a call from "my minister."

The disadvantages include: (a) the minister usually has a very busy Sunday morning schedule and does not gain the benefit of those very productive minutes for pastoral care on Sunday morning, (b) the minister may spend a very large amount of time traveling from one place to another, (c) for one or two of the congregations in the multi-church charge, the minister may provide only a maintenance level of service, (d) churches served by this arrangement tend not to be numerically growing congregations, (e) it may encourage an excessive emphasis on "Let's do more things together" in the interest of efficiency and reducing the workload on the minister, often at the cost of a lower level of participation, (f) it tends to produce brief pastorates, (g) sometimes it means one minister is expected to serve two congregations that are far apart on the theological spectrum and the only things they have in common are the geographical proximity of their meeting places and their inability to secure a full-time resident minister, (h) the arrangement tends to produce a low level of satisfaction for the minister since both the laity and the clergy tend to categorize these as second arrangements, and (i) the minister usually is not available to teach in the Sunday church school. This last objection is of major concern to those leaders who are convinced the church school is of central importance to church growth and who hold a strong pro-church growth position in regard to denominational strategy. (For additional reflections on this arrangement see question 4 in chapter 5.)

4. The retired minister

There was a day when most Christian ministers worked until they died, and many of those who did retire did so reluctantly because of health reasons.

Back in 1940, five years after the United States adopted the Social Security program with retirement set at age 65, the life expectancy of the average male was 61 years, and for the female it was 65 years. Today, it is 70 years for men and 77 years for women. Today, the average fifty-year-old man can expect to live another 25 years, and the average fifty-year-old woman can expect to live another 31 years.

One result of those changes is an increasing financial burden on the Social Security system and on private pension plans. Another is the increasing availability of ordained ministers who have retired from full-time service in the denomination, but who are not interested in full-time retirement.

For hundreds of small churches, when benefits are measured against costs, the most attractive alternative on this list will be to seek an officially retired minister who is interested in a three to seven-year pastorate in a small church.

5. The retired military chaplain

The 1980s will bring back into civilian life, after thirty years of service, a significant number of ordained ministers who entered the military service as chaplains during the Korean conflict. It also will bring back into civilian life a number of ordained ministers retiring after twenty years of service as chaplains, some of whom entered the service during the struggle in Vietnam.

Scores of small churches, and especially those in the Sunbelt, may want to consider this alternative as they look for their next pastor.

6. *The federated church*

This concept flourished during the second quarter of this century, but has received diminishing denominational support in recent years. The basic concept involves a programmatic and administrative merger of two or more congregations from different denominations, but with each member retaining his or her membership in the denomination of that person's choice. Thus the federation of three congregations usually produced one pastor, one governing board, one administrative structure, and one program structure, but three membership rosters and ties to three different denominational structures.

If and when there is a revival of interest in ecumenicity and/or interdenominational cooperation, there may be a revival of interest in this alternative.

Currently, however, many denominational leaders encourage congregations to enter into a federation only as a transitional stage in a congregational merger, following which the members will agree on an affiliation with one denomination.

7. *One congregation with two meeting places*

As church leaders discovered the depth of the pain felt by many members of churches when a merger forced them to give up the sacred building that had been their church home for decades, a new alternative surfaced. This is the product of an administrative merger that unites two or three congregations. The new congregation has one governing board, one pastor, one treasury, one set of officers, and one membership roll, but continues to maintain and use each of the buildings as a meeting place for worship, and, usually, for Sunday school. Typically, a different set of trustees is selected to care for each building. There are dozens of these arrangements in the Lutheran Church-Missouri Synod, The Christian Church (Disciples of Christ), and The United Presbyterian Church.

While only a small number of congregations have chosen this alternative, partly because of the cost of maintaining two meeting places; as the culture shifts from a functional to a relational set of values, it may attract the interest of more small churches, especially in the Sunbelt.

8. The yoked field

This resembles the multi-church parish or the circuit, but includes congregations from two or more different denominations. It is more common in sparsely populated areas and with congregations that have much in common and which often display only a modest degree of loyalty to their denomination.

The advantages include the opportunity to bring together two or three similar congregations that have much in common, the opportunity to share the cost of ministerial services, and the chance to take advantage of the geographical proximity of the meeting places.

The major disadvantages include the need for the minister to relate to two or three different denominations, and the confusion over denominational identity when "our new minister" comes from a different denomination.

9. The larger parish

This alternative has a large body of strong supporters in several denominations, and for thousands of small churches it is one of the most attractive options on this list.

While there are many variations on the basic concept, the typical arrangement includes three to ten small-town and rural churches. Each congregation retains its own autonomous role, maintains its own meeting place, plans and operates its own program, and has its own treasury. The cooperating churches, however, constitute a parish council, which is responsible for securing and relating to the program staff. Usually, but not always, the parish council administers a parish budget, based on contributions from the participating congregations, which provides the economic compensation for the paid staff, for central office expenses, and for some joint programming.[6]

Frequently the staff includes two to five professionals. One may specialize in Christian education for all of the participating congregations while also serving as the resident pastor of two or three congregations. Another may serve as staff director while also serving as the pastor of one or two congregations. A third might specialize in administration and finances while also serving as the pastor of two or three of the participating congregations. A fourth staff member may be a semiretired minister who preaches once or twice on Sunday and carries part of the pastoral load.

Among the many advantages of this alternative are that (a) it provides both staff generalists and specialists for each participating congregation, (b) it enables each minister to be a member of a mutual support group, (c) it offers the opportunity for each minister to be both a specialist and a generalist, (d) it reduces the sense of isolation that often undercuts the morale and the self-esteem of the small rural church, (e) it opens new doors to programming that no one congregation could initiate or staff with lay volunteers, (f) it provides new opportunities to challenge the creativity and commitment of the laity, (g) it enables some congregations to shift their priorities from institutional maintenance to mission and ministry, (h) it may create new opportunities to reach people who often are overlooked by most churches, and (i) sometimes it enables small-membership churches to attract and retain ministers who otherwise might not be interested in serving a small congregation.[7]

While this alternative has many very attractive features, it is not the easiest one to implement. Normally it requires (a) a willingness by some of the ablest, most widely respected and highly dedicated lay leaders from each congregation to serve on the parish council, (b) a highly skilled minister who is committed to the concept of cooperative ministries to serve as the parish director, (c) longer than average tenure by the staff, and (d) active support from the denominational leaders. It also usually means the staff must have a very influential role, and perhaps even the decisive voice, in selecting replacements when there is a change in staff. Naturally it also requires ministers who are committed to a collegial approach to the parish ministry and are reasonably secure people.

The larger parish rarely can, or should, be advocated as a means of saving money. Strengthening and expanding the ministry of the churches, not efficiency and economy, should be the criteria used by any congregation contemplating becoming a part of a larger parish.

There are several long-established larger parishes that have been developed across denominational lines and have functioned very effectively for many years. There is a tendency, however, for this concept to work more effectively in small-town and rural situations than in urban communities. One reason may be that more people have had more experience with cooperative ventures in rural America than in the cities. Another may be that the urban cooperative ministries have tended to focus on issue-centered ministries, rather than on staffing. (See question eight in chapter 5 for some other factors behind this distinction.)

10. *The pastor/associate minister arrangement*

One of the most effective approaches to staffing the small church to have emerged in recent years is one that responds to four needs in one package.

The basic ingredients of this alternative are (a) a congregation that is too large to be adequately staffed by one minister, but cannot afford or justify two pastors, (b) a small membership congregation (or perhaps two small churches) that need a part-time minister, but can neither afford nor justify a full-time pastor, (c) a minister who seeks the experience, challenge and opportunities of being a part-time program staff member in a larger church, but who also wants to be *the* pastor of "my own church where I have the full range of responsibilities," including the responsibility of preaching every Sunday morning, and (d) a senior minister in the large church who knows the difference between a full-time associate minister who is a generalist and a part-time program specialist, and prefers the latter.

When those four ingredients are put together, it can produce a minister who spends approximately half the time as program specialist in the larger congregation and is *the* pastor of the small (or the two small) congregation(s) that constitute the other half of this arrangement.

The critical variable in making this arrangement work over a period of several years is a very high degree of personal and professional compatibility between the two ministers who are involved. That does reduce the chances that every arrangement will be an overwhelming success! The major disadvantage is that the associate minister may be expected to spend sixty percent of his or her time in the larger church, while the smaller church(es) feel they are being cheated unlees they receive the benefit of at least 60 percent of their minister's time.

11. The use of trained lay leadership

One of the most promising alternatives on this list of alternatives for staffing the small-membership church is the greater use of trained lay leadership with an equivalent decrease in the traditional dependence on ordained ministers. There are at least four major variations on this theme.

One of them, pioneered by the Episcopal Church in Alaska, is to divide the professional responsibilities of the ordained minister into separate responsibilities and to train lay persons to carry out their responsibilities. One lay person, for example, might be trained to serve as the preacher for that congregation, another as the sacramentalist, a third as the educator, a fourth as the person responsible for the pastoral care of the members, and a fifth as the administrator.

This approach requires a strong commitment by the leadership in the regional judicatory to a ministry of the laity, competent leadership to train the laity, and a high level of personal and professional security that enables the ordained ministers to freely surrender some of the authority traditionally reserved to the clergy.

A second approach is to deploy trained lay persons, under the continuing supervision of a neighboring ordained minister, to serve as the pastors of a small congregation. A few denominations, such as The United Methodist Church, have a polity and a history that makes this a very attractive alternative. In some of the strongly congregational polity denominations there are reservations about this, because of the lack of a denominational structure that would reinforce the supervisor-pastor relationship.

Usually that lay minister serves only one or two congregations and is compensated on a part-time basis.

One version of this approach has the supervising

minister, who is also the full-time pastor of a 400-member church, serving as "the senior minister" of the small church; and the lay person who carries nearly all of the actual work load is identified as the "associate minister" of that congregation. In this particular example, the supervising minister serves as the moderator of the monthly meeting of the Session, preaches in the church twice a year, supervises the associate minister's ministry, and occasionally conducts a funeral, officiates at a wedding, or makes a hospital call on a member of that congregation. The congregation pays its "senior minister" $600 a year, and pays the part-time "associate minister" $4,200 annually—and receives a total of at least $7,000 or $8,000 in ministerial services from this two-person team.

A third approach to the use of the laity, and one that has hundreds of years of history behind it, is for the congregation to set apart one of its members to serve as the minister. Sometimes that person is paid, and sometimes that set-apart minister serves in a volunteer role. The Mennonites, Brethren, and Friends have a rich history in this approach that deserves the scrutiny of leaders from other denominational families.

A contemporary version of this approach can be found in many churches, both urban and rural, in which a team of lay persons covenant together to carry the responsibilities normally assigned to a paid minister. (This concept also has come back into use in many larger congregations for six to twelve weeks while the minister takes an official leave of absence for graduate work, for major surgery, to give birth to a baby, or to take an extended study travel leave.)

A fourth approach, which sometimes is not perceived as being in this category, is the widely used idea of licensing the preseminary college student to serve as the minister of a small congregation on a part-time basis while still in college. Tens of thousands of today's pastors began their ministerial careers while serving as lay ministers of small congregations while in college or seminary.

12. *The service bureau*

While it has been limited to a handful of experimental ventures, the last alternative on this list deserves a brief mention here, because it could be a much larger part of tomorrow's world.

Basically it involves the creation by a regional judicatory, or by a group ministry, of a central service bureau to which congregations can come and purchase ministerial services. Some may want only a preacher for the Sunday morning worship service. Others may want a minister who will teach an adult class and also conduct the Sunday morning service. Certain churches will want a minister both for Sunday morning and for Sunday evening services. Occasionally a church will come to the service for a preacher to fill in on Sunday morning while their pastor recovers from an illness. Another congregation may be seeking a part-time interim minister to fill in while they seek a full-time replacement for their pastor who resigned a few weeks earlier. A few churches may come looking for a permanent part-time pastor. The congregation decides on the size of the package of the ministerial services it wants and is willing to pay for and pays the service bureau for these services. This bureau brings together resources and matches them with needs.

In addition to the ordained minister who is the director of the bureau, the staff might include a semi-retired minister who wants only to preach on Sundays, one or two seminary interns, a couple of ordained ministers who teach in college or in a theological seminary, two or three trained lay preachers, a hospital chaplain who is available on Sunday mornings, a member of the staff of the regional judicatory of the sponsoring denomination, a retired military chaplain, three or four ordained ministers with full-time secular jobs, or the pastor of a small congregation who is available for certain responsibilities during the week. (If this staff also includes the part-time services of a person who has a full-time night shift job, this can be very beneficial in developing responses to the growing number of rural residents who work nights.)

From this team the director assigns a member to preach at church A, another person to preach and also be responsible for all the funerals and weddings at church B, someone to serve as the one-third-time pastor of church C, and a person to work with the Christian education committee at church D.

While this is a highly functional approach to staffing churches in what is an increasingly relational world, it merits consideration if (a) the concept has the unreserved support of the regional judicatory of that denomination, (b) it is assumed that, within a year, or two at the most, this will become a financially self-supporting venture and not simply serve as a channel for indirect subsidies to small churches, (c) it is staffed with a creative, personable, and aggressive director, and (d) an effort is made to develop a strong relationship between the team member assigned to a particular congregation and the members of that church—excessive rotation of staff members can be destructive, and relationships do need to be nurtured.

While this list of a dozen different alternative approaches to providing ministerial leadership for small-membership churches is not intended to be an exhaustive review of all the alternatives, it does reinforce the point that the basic choice is *not* between "our own full-time minister or closing." There are many other alternatives on the list. That raises the question of assigning the responsibility for choosing among these various alternatives.

D. Who Will Make That Choice?

The Washington Avenue Church had been organized in 1923 to serve the residents of what, at that time, was a new residential neighborhood about three miles west of the center of the city. Old First Church, with a meeting place in the heart of downtown, had initiated the idea, and 34 members left First Church to form the nucleus of this new congregation. For the first thirty years of its life, the new congregation led a precarious existence. A motion at a congregational meeting in 1933 to dissolve and rejoin First Church lost by a 36 to 39 vote.

During the nineteen-fifties, however, the church prospered. Membership peaked at 499 in 1957. A new educational wing was completed in 1963. By 1973 it became obvious the bloom was off the rose, and the average attendance at Sunday morning worship was down to 110. A disastrous pastorate in the mid-1970s resulted in another sharp drop in participation. A vigorous new pastor arrived in 1977 and brought new hope to some of the leaders, but when that minister soon moved on to another pastorate, the numbers began to decline.

Recently, when that minister's successor resigned and left rather suddenly, the leaders arranged to bring in two different outside "experts" to advise them on their situation.

The meeting with the first one closed with the outsider offering these words of counsel. "It appears to me you have four alternatives. One is to vote to dissolve. A second is to initiate the process of merging with some other congregation, perhaps with First Church. A third is to postpone the day of reckoning for a few more years by seeking a part-time pastor, perhaps a retired minister, who will fill the pulpit for you. The fourth is to pray for at least a medium-sized miracle."

109

The Small Church Is Different!

A few weeks later, the leaders met with a staff member from the denominational headquarters. About halfway through that evening's discussion, the denominational staffer suggested, "It seems to me that the central question here is, 'How do we strengthen, reinforce, and expand the ministry and outreach of this congregation today and tomorrow?' Given the nature, history, and traditions of this church, that probably means the next step is to find a minister to fill the current vacancy here. Let's take some time now and build a list of alternatives open to you in securing ministerial leadership for the next several years."

An hour later, the group had created a list of nine different alternatives. The first one on the list was a seminary-trained, full-time resident minister. It was noted this probably would require $7,000 to $10,000 annually in financial aid from the denomination, and that aid might not be available. After a brief discussion of the pros and cons of each alternative, the staff member suggested, "Now, before we leave, why don't you folks set a date when you will meet again, perhaps two or three more times, and review these alternatives. You may think of alternatives you want to add to the list. After you have reviewed them, select the three that are most attractive to you. Rank those three in your order of preference. List opposite each one what you will need from the denomination in order to implement that alternative. For example, if you decide an attractive alternative would be to seek a retired military chaplain, we can put you in touch with the office that can provide a list of possibilities. Now, lest there be any misunderstanding, I will wait to hear from you. The next move is up to you. I will not do anything on this until after you contact me again."

As they left that meeting, one of the long-time members of the Washington Avenue Church said to the person giving him a ride home, "I was kind of disappointed with tonight's meeting. I was expecting someone would come in and tell us what to do next, or at least promise to find a new minister for us."

"No, that's not the way it is anymore," replied the driver. "It's now up to us to decide what we want to do. We'll have to live with the consequences of what happens next, so I guess we should accept the responsibility of making the decision. To tell you the truth, I sort of long for the old days when we could go to the denomination and ask them to help us find a minister, but I guess it's better this way. Can you drive or do you want me to pick you up for next week's meeting?"

Chapter IV

THE SUNDAY
CHURCH SCHOOL

I wish somebody would publish a curriculum series designed for small churches like ours," sighed Becky Henderson at the monthly Saturday morning meeting of the Christian education committee of the 138-member Trinity Church. "It seems to me one of the church supply houses would design a curriculum for small churches."

"I really don't like any of these," added Ruth Johnson. "This group-graded series would be all right if it had more Bible in it. I like the design, but not the content."

"Well, let's stop complaining and make a choice," urged the minister. "Last month you asked me to order some more samples and promised that we would make a choice today. We have to get the order in the mail this next week."

That same evening, Becky Henderson and her husband were enjoying their monthly social get-together with three other couples from Trinity Church. Halfway through their dinner, the conversation drifted into some nostalgic recollections about the Sunday school. "My best memories of the years I spent in Sunday school as a kid are of Mrs. White," recalled one of the men. "She was my teacher for four years, and she was a wonderful person. She was born and reared on a farm, married to a farmer and spent her whole life on a farm. I doubt if she ever finished high school, but she knew the Bible. More important, however, she loved every one of us. She didn't have any kids of her own, but she was a living example of God's love for each of his children."

"What I remember most clearly was good old Mr. Churchill. He was a pretty strict old fellow," recalled another husband, "but he loved to teach our class. Those were the days when there were boys' classes and girls' classes. He taught our class of high school boys. He was really a saint, and I know some of us boys tried to model ourselves after Mr. Churchill."

"The most important thing I got out of Sunday school as a youngster was the chance to associate with Mrs. Ellis," reflected Becky Henderson. "She had a greater impact on my life than any other person I knew in my childhood. A few years ago I wrote her a note thanking her for all she had done for me, but it came back marked 'Addressee deceased.' I sure wish I had thanked her while she was still alive."

These two conversations reflect one of the most important characteristics of the Sunday church school. The generalization applies to churches of all sizes, but is especially applicable to small congregations. *To a very substantial degree the teacher is the curriculum.* The most influential decisions on the curriculum are made in the selection of the teachers, not in the selection of printed materials.[1] This point can be illustrated by asking a large group of today's adults this question, "If you attended Sunday school on a regular basis as a child, what is your best, most favorable, and happiest recollection of that experience?" Typically a majority of those responding will identify and affirm a relationship with an adult. A smaller group will mention a specific experience or event. Another group of approximately the same size will describe a specific experience that reinforced that individual's identity as a person in his or her own right. A somewhat smaller group usually will recall with great pleasure an experience that enabled them to display their creative gifts. Typically, only three to five percent or less will place the highest priority on the recollection of some cognitive or factual learning.

"We always have Sunday school every Sunday morning," explained a long-time member of a Baptist congregation in a rural section of Tennessee, "and now we have a preaching service on the first and third Sundays of every month. When I was a boy here, we only had preaching services once a month."

"You're asking about our average attendance," replied the pastor of an open country church. "It's right up there on the wall. You see that wooden signboard with the cardboard numbers on it? It says attendance today was 51, last Sunday was 48, and a year ago was 52. Is that precise enough for you?"

"That's the Sunday school attendance, isn't it?" questioned the visitor. "I was asking about your average attendance at worship."

"Oh, golly, I'm not sure exactly what that is," replied the minister. "Nobody counts that, but I guess it would be somewhere between thirty-five and sixty."

"My predecessor tried to close that little church about four years ago," explained the United Methodist District Superintendent. "He figured they would be willing to talk about closing if they didn't have a preacher, so he left them without a minister for two years. It didn't faze them. They kept right on as they had always been. Sometimes they found someone to come in and conduct a preaching service. Some Sundays the Sunday school superintendent did it. On a good many Sundays all they had was Sunday school. When I came on the district, I found a minister who is serving a church in a town north of here who was willing to come down every Sunday morning and conduct the worship service. Back when they were part of a three-point circuit, they averaged 18 to 20 at worship. Today they average 18 to 20 at worship with about 25 in the Sunday school."

"The Builders' Class is the real powerhouse in this congregation," explained the pastor of a 135-member ex-neighborhood church in a city of 100,000 residents. "Nearly all of our leaders come out of the Builders' Class.

Whatever that class wants to happen, does happen. If the pastor doesn't have their support, he might as well pack up and leave."

"Sounds like that's a group to be reckoned with," replied the visitor.

"Yes, it is," agreed the minister. "I've always been able to get along with that class ever since I came here. I've even been asked to teach it a couple of times when their regular teacher was out of town. My biggest complaint about it is that only about half of the members of the Builders' Class come to church regularly. The other half never miss that class, but, except for Christmas, Easter, Mother's Day, and maybe one or two other times a year, they never come to worship. That gives me problems."

"We can schedule the worship service at either 8:30 or 11:00," declared a member of the 83-member Oak Grove Church, "but we can't take the 9:45 hour. Our Sunday school has always met at ten, and I don't believe our people would be willing to change that." This statement was part of a conversation when representatives of the Oak Grove Church were meeting with members of two other congregations to discuss the possibility of the three churches' sharing the services of the same minister.

These five conversations illustrate what may be the most significant characteristic of the Sunday church school in thousands of small churches. It is the center of the organizational life. This generalization especially applies to most small congregations in several denominations, such as the Christian Church (Disciples of Christ), United Methodist, Southern Baptist, Nazarene, and others with a strong adult Sunday school tradition. It is less likely to apply to churches in the Reformed, Lutheran, and Anglican traditions. In these denominations, the minister and the corporate worship experience tend to constitute the hub of congregational life. The centrality of the Sunday school in so many small churches, however, is a factor whose importance should not be minimized.

"We need to be thinking about finding someone to replace Mr. Burke as the teacher of the adult class," suggested Mrs. Harris to other members of the Sunday school board at the Park Church.

"Why? Is he thinking of retiring?" inquired another member. "I realize he's been teaching that class since the later 1950s, but he's only 63 or 64 and he's still very sharp and vigorous. Why should we be thinking about replacing him?"

"Well, he brought it up the other day when we were talking," explained Mrs. Harris. "He pointed out that most of the people under forty who could be in that class, aren't in it. Some are teaching, but there's at least a half-dozen others who could and should be in it. Mr. Burke suggested that if we could find a younger person to teach it, we might be able to attract these younger adults."

"What happened in the high school class?" Mrs. Sinclair asked of her seventeen-year-old daughter.

"I don't know. I wasn't there. Starting today, I'm helping Mrs. Buckner with the intermediate class," replied the daughter. "She celebrated her seventieth birthday last Tuesday and decided she's ready for some help with those little kids, so from now on, I'll be helping her."

"The Sunday after I graduated from high school, I came into Mr. Engle's Men's Bible Class," recalled the sixty-three-year-old Sam McKay. "When Mr. Engle died, back in 1959, they asked me to take over for him, and I've been teaching the class ever since."

These three conversations illustrate another distinctive characteristic of the Sunday church school in many small churches, and one of its major assets. It is intergenerational.

There is a widespread, and, by the value system of this

observer, a very unfortunate tendency to encourage the Sunday church school in small-membership churches to be a small-scale model of the closely graded Sunday school operated by large congregations.

A far better approach is to affirm the distinctive strengths, resources, and assets of the church school in the small congregation, and seek to build on these assets. This raises five questions for the agenda of the small-membership church.

These questions should be examined in the light of these three distinctive characteristics of the Sunday church school in the typical small church. First, the teacher is the most important component of the curriculum, especially for children, but also for all ages. Second, the Sunday school is often the central factor in the organizational life of the small congregation. Third, in most small churches, the Sunday school operates on an intergenerational model. Now let us turn to these five questions.

A. What Are Our Goals?

The first question concerns the purpose of the goals of the church school. Why continue it? What is its purpose? What are the goals?

In the opening chapter of her excellent book on Christian education, Iris Cully emphasizes the critical importance of widespread agreement on goals. She goes on to suggest that the Bible, commitment, belief, affirmation of the church, or a way of life may be the central theme of the Sunday school. The choice matters little. What does matter is that the minister, the parents, the teachers, the people enrolled in the Sunday school, the congregational leaders, and those preparing the curriculum must agree on the central goal before they will be able to develop an effective Sunday school.[2]

The Small Church Is Different!

In some small rural churches, a widely shared hope is that the children will grow up and not move away. Some people believe the Sunday school could be a factor in this. Others want the Sunday school to inculcate a strong church loyalty so that when these children do grow up and move away, they will continue as active church members. In many small city churches, the Sunday school is perceived as a means of reaching neighborhood children who, it is hoped, will grow up and become replacement members for those members who move away or die, and/or become a channel for reaching the parents of these children.

In many churches of all sizes, both urban and rural, many parents believe the number-one goal of the Sunday school should be to teach children the content of the Bible. In others, developing a strong denominational loyalty is the primary goal. In a few, the emphasis on missions tops the list of goals. In a growing number of small-membership churches, the Sunday school is perceived as the most important single channel for reaching and attracting the new generation of young parents born after World War II.

As Mrs. Cully suggests, the first step in developing a good Sunday church school is to secure widespread agreement on goals. Until that agreement has been reached, it will be very difficult to develop a specific program to implement the goals. The centrality of the Sunday school in thousands of small-membership churches means these goals will have a profound, long-term impact on all other aspects of ministry and outreach of that congregation.

B. What Is the Role of Young People and Adults?

In many congregations it is widely assumed that children are the primary clients of the Sunday school. When that is true, it raises questions about the role of young people and adults. In most churches, the teenagers teach children one of three lessons in regard to the Sunday school.

In some congregations the teenagers drop out of Sunday school following confirmation, or at about the ninth or tenth grade. Thus, by their actions they teach younger children that Sunday school is for women and children, and that when a person reaches adolescence, the appropriate behavior pattern is to drop out of Sunday school.

In other churches, teenagers, and especially teenage girls, do not attend a high school class. Instead, they teach or help teach a class of children. This behavior pattern reinforces the image that Sunday school is for women and children, and/or affirms the concept that teaching is more important than learning, and/or the idea that the teachers are the primary clients of the Sunday school and the pupils are secondary clients. A child learns to look forward to being promoted to the day when "I can be a teacher or a helper."

In many small churches, however, the high school class is an exciting experience that attracts six to ten or more teenagers every Sunday morning. By their presence, their interest, their conversation, and their actions as role models, these teenagers are teaching younger children that Sunday school is important and that it can be a creative and enriching experience. What are the teenagers teaching the children in your congregation?

A parallel question can be asked about adults. There is a large and growing school of thought that suggests the most influential teaching by adults is done through modeling behavior. The most effective method of producing an adult who smokes cigarettes is to have that person grow up in a home in which one or both parents smoke. The most effective method of teaching a child to learn to read and to enjoy reading is to have that child grow up in a home in which one or both parents spend large amounts of time reading and in which the older siblings are bookworms. The most effective means of producing an active, church-going adult Roman Catholic is to have that person grow up as a child in a home in which at least one parent goes to Mass at least once a week.[3]

When translated into implications for the small-membership church, the concept of teaching through modeling means that adult behavior is very influential. Perhaps the best beginning point for strengthening the children's division is to have at least one male-dominated* adult Sunday school class meeting in a very conspicuous place, so the children can see that participation in Sunday school is appropriate behavior for adults.

If adults teach by who they are and by what they do, an adult class may be the critical element in developing a strong Sunday school in the small congregation. Many pastors of small-membership churches affirm this concept by teaching the adult class during the Sunday school hour.

This emphasis on modeling can be reinforced by scheduling ten or fifteen minutes for the "opening exercises," with active participation by all ages. This time should include singing one or two hymns that children can appreciate, a recognition of birthdays and other special events that reinforce the distinctive identity of each person, as well as a time of intercessory prayer, a brief meditation, and announcements concerning the special mission of that Sunday school.

C. What Is the Place of the Sunday School?

In hundreds of large churches, the Sunday church school is but one component of a larger educational program. The

---

*Males tend to model behavior patterns, while females tend to be more influential in modeling beliefs.

educational program is but one of several subcommunities
that include the ministry of music, the youth program, the
women's organization, missions, the recreational program,
and community ministries. The Sunday school is but one
room in that fifteen-room house.

By contrast, in thousands of small-membership churches,
corporate worship and Sunday school constitute the basic
program of that congregation. In several denominations it is
not unusual for the attendance at Sunday school to exceed
that at worship for a large proportion of the congregations.

What is the place of the Sunday school in your
congregation? If it is central, you may want to reinforce that
central role. Among the ways this is done in small churches
is to (a) assign the choice hour on Sunday morning to the
Sunday school; (b) recognize that the only active standing
program committee will be the Sunday school board or the
Christian education committee; (c) affirm the office of
Sunday school superintendent as the most important lay
office in that congregation; (d) encourage the Sunday school
to have its own treasury, treasurer, and special mission
project; (e) expect that all of the costs for materials,
curriculum, and supplies will be paid out of the Sunday
school treasury; (f) assume that the Sunday school will be
responsible for certain all-church programs, such as the
Christmas Eve service, the presentation of a religious
drama, the annual homecoming celebration, the annual
picnic, and/or the special Thanksgiving service; (g) organize
a Sunday school choir—or better yet, a Sunday school
orchestra; (h) be sure there is at least one strong adult class
with an excellent teacher;[4] (i) schedule Rally Day and/or
Promotion Sunday as a major event in the church year; (j)
encourage older teenagers to be active leaders in the Sunday
school organization; and (k) schedule one major continuing
education event each year for teachers and officers.

One reason we know these are critical factors in

reinforcing the central role of the Sunday school is that those who have sought to downgrade its role have found these to be points of vulnerability in reducing the influence of the Sunday school.

D. What Is the Hidden Curriculum?

Several years ago, a psychiatrist wrote a very provocative book in which he contended, "I have found that a hidden curriculum determines, to a significant degree, what becomes the basis for all participants' sense of worth and self-esteem." He pointed out, for example, that most university students discover within a few weeks following the beginning of the term that they cannot complete all of the assigned work. As a result, the student learns to cope with these excessive expectations by learning selective neglect—which assignments should be largely ignored.[5] That learning is part of the hidden curriculum.

What is the hidden curriculum in your Sunday school? What are the children being taught? How to survive until they are old enough to drop out? How to please the teacher? That Sunday school is a place to teach children to obey adults? Does it teach children that our church is the only sure road to salvation? That adults do not agree on how to interpret the Bible? That the Bible is a book to be memorized? That the Sunday school is a competitor with the worship hour? That children attend Sunday school and adults participate in worship?

Or does the hidden curriculum include the transmission of the congregational history, values, traditions, legends, folklore, and other forces that have been central to the distinctive identity of that parish? Does the hidden curriculum help children and teenagers understand why we continue as a worshiping congregation? Does the hidden curriculum reinforce family ties and help children understand their roots more adequately? Does the hidden curriculum reinforce a particular doctrinal stance? Does the hidden curriculum reinforce an environment in which people can both share and grow in their faith? Does the hidden curriculum lift up the centrality of worship? Does it help people see the congregation as an interdependent part of the universal church? Does the hidden curriculum reinforce the importance of affection, of community building, of story telling, of role models, of spiritual mentors, of experiencing the faith, and of prayer? That is what made the Sunday school the force it was for more than a century!

What is the hidden curriculum in your Sunday church school?

E. What Are the Advantages?

The last of these five questions on the Sunday church school overlaps a variety of issues, ranging from congregational self-esteem, to planning, to pedagogical styles. The question is a simple one. What are the unique advantages of the small-membership church in developing an educational program? The Christian education committee in one 85-member congregation took an hour one evening to reflect on that question and came up with these responses.

"One advantage we have is that we have a higher proportion of our members involved in Sunday school than the big churches have," commented one member. "It's easier for us to make changes and adapt to new circumstances," offered another. "People have more chances to participate here, we need everyone," added a third member of the committee. "Everyone is treated as an individual here." "Everybody knows everyone else by name." "It's easier to recruit teachers." "We have a better support system for the whole Sunday school than you can find in most big churches." "Ours is lay-run. We don't depend on paid staff like the big churches." "It's naturally intergenerational." "There is a greater sense of caring." "We don't need as much space, and we make more efficient use of the limited space we do have." "We have better communication among all the teachers and leaders." "It costs less." "We have a more informal and less complex administrative structure." "There's more interest in it." "We're forced to be creative." "Everyone feels needed." "It's easier to build and maintain important traditions." "The adults are highly visible and readily accessible as adult role models for the children and youth." "The adults feel and benefit from the vitality of the children and youth who are close by." "Our Sunday school is an easy place for newcomers to gain a sense of belonging." "We reinforce the sense of intergenerational obligation rather than isolate generations from one another." "Learning is within the context of caring." "It runs without the pastor." "We have lots of peer-group teaching." "The students, not the teachers, are the primary clients." "We have a greater degree of continuity among the teachers." "We are more open to the shy, the bashful, and the introverted." "We don't classify people by their marital status." "The whole program is within the context of the family and reinforces family ties."

What special advantages does the Sunday school enjoy in your congregation?

Chapter V

TEN QUESTIONS

I f you ask me, we already have too many churches," declared the senior minister of a large downtown church. "Why should we be starting more churches when we already have too many? Why not invest that time and money in helping some of these small churches to merge? A lot of them will close in the next ten years if something isn't done."

"Well, we may not have to start a lot of new congregations," replied a denominational staff member. "At the rate people are moving out of the central cities and older suburban communities to the rural counties, we may be glad we have all those small rural churches out there to serve that new migration."

"From what I've seen, I'm not sure you can count on some of those churches' reaching the newcomers," observed a pastor who was a part of the conversation. "When a minister is serving two or three of those small churches, it's pretty hard to have the time left to court new people. Besides, a lot of the people moving to the rural areas today are making that move in order to get more privacy. They want to be left alone. They aren't looking for some preacher to come knocking on their door."

"Well, we're sure feeling the effects of that migration to exurbia," commented the pastor of a shrinking central-city congregation. "We've had a dozen families move out in the last couple of years, but they now live too far out to come back in to church. I guess we'll have to see if Bethany Church would be interested in merging with us."

"Why merge?" inquired another member of the group. "Why go through all the agonies of a merger? Why don't you folks, Bethany, and the Cleveland Avenue Church get together and do more joint programming? That would be easier than a merger and a lot more effective."

This conversation lifts up several of the questions that come up repeatedly when the discussion moves to the future of the small-membership church. Are there too many churches? What will be the impact of the new urban-rural migration? How can one minister serve a two or three-church parish? Should some of these small congregations get together and merge? Will many die during the next several years? Or should the emphasis be on cooperative programming? Perhaps the most productive approach would be to examine these and related questions one by one. The first one is a question that is asked thousands of times every year.

A. Are There Too Many Churches?

In 1980, City Planner Rick Kuckkahn urged the Planning Commission of New Berlin, Wisconsin, to limit the number of churches to one for every 2,500 residents. He argued that permitting too many congregations to construct buildings might be unwise and that each church should include a minimum of twenty-five families. As part of his argument, Mr. Kuckkahn cited the Wisconsin Council of Churches' guideline of an optimum ratio of one church for every 2,500 residents.[1]

Fifty years earlier, several national church leaders had urged a ratio of one congregation for every thousand residents in rural America. When this ratio was applied to South Dakota, and its 693,000 residents, the result was an "excess" of 1196 congregations. The actual ratio was one congregation for each 367 residents, and this probably understated the situation since that census of churches was less than complete.

An admittedly incomplete survey of the churches in the city and county of Roanoke, Virginia, in the winter of 1957-58, found a total of 164 congregations serving a population of 160,000—and counted only those congregations that could be contacted by telephone.[2] A comprehensive study of Summit County, Ohio, including the City of Akron, conducted in 1963-64, identified 564 religious congregations, each with its own meeting place, serving a population of 525,000 residents.[3] Fort Wayne, Indiana, is one of scores of communities frequently referred to as "the city of churches," and two out of five church members are Roman Catholic. Fort Wayne has 200 congregations for 180,000 residents. In several predominantly Protestant cities in the southeastern section of the United States, there is one religious congregation for every 500 to 600 residents.

The more than 250 religious bodies in the United States report a combined total of approximately 350,000 churches. When an allowance is made for the growing number of house churches, independent congregations, and other groups that do not get counted, there is probably one religious congregation for every 400 to 500 residents. The ratio varies from one congregation for every 150 to 200 residents in some rural counties in the South, to one congregation for every 300 to 500 residents in rural counties in the North, to one for every 1000 residents in many northern urban counties.[4] In Canada there is *at least* one religious congregation for every 900 residents, and the ratio probably is closer to one for each 750.

Could people be better served by fewer congregations? For at least six decades, many of the professional leaders in American Protestantism have given a resounding "Yes!" to that question. Perhaps the best longitudinal study that speaks to this issue was conducted in Muncie, Indiana. In their pioneering study, *Middletown*, conducted in 1924, Robert and Helen Lynd found that only a quarter of all married couples in Muncie went to church. In 1978, approximately one half of all married couples in Muncie were regular churchgoers. The number of church buildings in Muncie increased from one for every 870 residents in 1924 to one for every 538 in 1978.[5] While no one has proved the cause and effect relationship, those places with a relatively large number of churches per one thousand residents usually have a higher proportion of churchgoers than those places with a very low ratio of churches to population— New York City, San Francisco, and Columbia, Maryland, are examples of a low church-to-population ratio and of a low proportion of churchgoers.

In broad general terms, there are seven statements that should be considered when someone suggests there are too many churches in a particular community.

1. Second thoughts on this subject

First, as was pointed out earlier, the proportion of churchgoers in the population tends to be higher in those communities in which there is at least one church per thousand residents and lower where there is less than one church per thousand residents.

Second, the "successful" efforts to control or reduce the number of churches in a community usually have been followed by a surprisingly low proportion of churchgoers in the population.

Third, congregational mergers usually result in a decrease in the number of churchgoers. (See question 9 below.)

Fourth, those denominations that have achieved a significant reduction in the total number of congregations also have experienced a sharp decline in membership and worship attendance. (The United Church of Christ, The United Methodist Church, and the Christian Church [Disciples of Christ] are three outstanding examples of this pattern.)

Fifth, those denominations that have achieved a sharp *increase* in the number of congregations also have experienced a major increase in the membership. (The Southern Baptist Convention and the Mormons are two of the most highly visible illustrations of this pattern.)

Sixth, new congregations are more likely to reach people without an active church relationship than are long-established churches.

Seventh, those communities that have experienced a sharp increase in the number of churches per 1000 residents usually have experienced a significant increase in the proportion of churchgoers in the population.

Instead of trying to make people feel guilty over an "excess" of churches, the real need may be to increase the number of congregations with an active, aggressive, and imaginative evangelistic outreach!

B. What Keeps All of These Little Churches Going?

Back in the 1950s, hundreds of small congregations were warned, "An examination of the age distribution of your membership suggests this congregation will die off in another fifteen or twenty years," or "This community has more people moving out than are moving in and it is doubtful there will be a place for this church twenty years from now," or "The consolidation of the public schools makes it inevitable that there will be a consolidation of churches."

The most comprehensive longitudinal study of the rural church scene ever completed studied the churches in 99 rural townships in Missouri in 1952 and again in 1967. The consolidation of rural schools, the decline in the number and strength of other rural institutions, the drop in the population, the emergence of larger trade centers, and other factors caused the researchers to anticipate a sharp decline in the number of churches in these 99 townships. What did they find?

Out of the 534 congregations that had existed in these 99 rural townships in 1952, only 69 had ceased to exist by 1967. (The loss rate was highest, largely through mergers, in those denominations with a strong centralized or connectional polity. The Presbyterians saw 6 out of their 25 churches close during that fifteen-year period while Methodists lost 20 out of 95. By contrast, only 4 out of 53 Disciples of Christ and 6 out of 123 Southern Baptist congregations ceased to exist.) All told, the losses, which averaged less than one percent per year,* were partially offset by the emergence of 46 new congregations, an average of three per year. The researchers concluded these rural churches displayed a remarkable ability to survive in a situation that appeared to be very unfavorable for survival![6]

Why? What makes the small church such a tough institution?

There are at least eight major factors that influence the capability of the small church to survive. Some of these can be identified most clearly in studies of rural churches in sparsely populated counties, while others are more visible in small, inner-city congregations in large metropolitan communities.

1. It's not a branch office!

Perhaps the most overlooked factor is that the local church is not a branch office! It is not an integral part of a

---

*The death rate for the American people is 0.9 percent per year. A variety of studies and surveys suggest the annual "death rate" for churches via mergers, dissolutions, and closings of all types is approximately 0.8 percent, but it may be as high as 1.2 percent.

larger social system. It is basically an autonomous and independent primary group.

This distinction escaped those who saw the school consolidation efforts of the 1940-70 era as a forerunner of what inevitably would overtake the churches.[7]

Unlike the public schools, the worshiping congregation's role and future are not subject to standards and orders issued from a central authority. As long as the congregation continues as a primary group for the members, it will continue to be an institutionally tough organization. The more it becomes subject to standards, values, goals, and directions determined by regional and national agencies, the more fragile it will become. This is one of the basic reasons why sect-type, isolationist, and inward-looking congregations tend to have a higher survival rate than mission-oriented and denomination-related churches.

2. It reinforces community

A second factor is that as long as a congregation continues to be a strong force in reinforcing community identity, in undergirding the sense of community, and in clarifying the individual's roots, it will tend to have a high survival record.[8]

One of the places this factor can be seen very clearly is in the institutional strength and high survival rate of Protestant (both black and white), Catholic, and Jewish congregations in cities such as New York, Akron, Detroit, Milwaukee, Minneapolis, Omaha, Cleveland, and Chicago, where the church often was a strong integrative force among recently arrived immigrants from Poland, Sweden, Hungary, Holland, Russia, Italy, West Virginia, Mississippi, Kentucky, or Alabama. When those congregations began to lose their influence as expressions and reinforcements of a distinctive community identity, they became institutionally more fragile. Another place this same phenomenon can be seen is in what once were very strong German Lutheran or Dutch Reformed rural communities in Michigan or Iowa. The more a congregation expresses and reinforces a distinctive community identity, the greater its institutional strength.

3. Subsidies increase vulnerability

A third factor is one that applies to all social institutions. As long as an individual, institution, or organization can remain economically self-sufficient and be largely independent of a larger organizational structure, it will tend to be relatively invulnerable to any external pressures that might force it to close or cause it to disband.

Examples of this generalization include the self-sufficient Amish farmer, the independent auto mechanic who operates his own garage, the "Mom and Pop" independent grocery store; and the small rural congregation that meets in a thrifty small building, is served by a part-time minister who is a self-employed and independent farmer, and has no other payroll obligations.

By contrast, the service station operator who staffs a station owned by a major oil company, the small church that receives a substantial financial subsidy from the denomination, or the branch office of a major conglomerate are institutionally more fragile. In general, financial dependence and institutional vulnerability go together in today's world.

4. The socialization factor

The fourth of these eight factors can be stated in a question. Who socializes whom?

In the small-town church, the minister often brings a world-view that is not native to that community, but frequently the congregation socializes the new minister to local values, traditions, and customs.[9] In general, the more the minister accepts, affirms, endorses, and supports the values, traditions, and background of the congregation, the lower the level of institutional vulnerability of the congregation. By contrast, the more successful the minister is in socializing the long-established congregation to accept that pastor's values, standards, criteria for self-evaluation, and goals, the less likely that congregation will be in existence twenty years hence. This second generalization can be illustrated by examining the life, ministry, and eventual termination of scores of churches in large central cities where the neighborhood context changed from very supportive to hostile. The church that functions in a strongly supportive community context (see question 3 below) often can survive the efforts of the pastor to socialize that congregation to the minister's world-view, values, and goals. If, however, the community setting is on the hostile side of neutral, those efforts may prove fatal to the congregation.

5. *The importance of shared experiences*

A fifth source of institutional strength for the small congregation, and especially the long-established small church with a distinctive language, nationality, racial, or ethnic identity, is the emphasis on shared experiences. These shared experiences include funeral services, weddings, baptisms, christenings, money-making activities, construction programs, picnics, social occasions, homecomings, and special holy days. The greater the number and variety of these events that have a high percentage of participation by the members, the greater the institutional tenacity.

This is one reason why the small church that affirms a

variety of shared experiences, such as opening exercises in the Sunday school, the annual homecoming weekend, the big Christmas Eve program, and similar events, tends to be an institutionally tougher congregation than the identical size church that has minimized the importance of shared experiences.

6. The centrality of worship

The sixth cohesive force that is of distinctive significance for the small-membership church is that it focuses most of its resources on a single theme—it is a community of believers where people come together to worship God and to love and care for one another. It is built around the two great commandments of Jesus (Matthew 22:39-40). This is the greatest single source of the institutional strength of the typical small church.[10] By contrast, many larger congregations spread their resources over a wide range of ministries, causes, needs, specialized staff, and service programs. The greater the range and scope of program, the stronger the evangelistic outreach—and the greater the institutional vulnerability of the congregation. (That is a tradeoff many church leaders do not like to recognize.) In most small churches, by contrast, worship and the church school constitute the heart of the program.

7. The role of the laity

A seventh factor that helps to explain the unexpectedly high survival rate among small-membership churches is that they tend to be lay-dominated institutions. This characteristic is more prevalent in rural churches than in urban congregations, which tend to be more dependent on the pastor as a cohesive and unifying force.

In general, the stronger the role of the laity, the greater

the institutional strength of a congregation.* The greater the reliance on the minister as the central organizing force, the more vulnerable the congregation, and especially the more likely it is that a change in pastoral leadership will turn out to be disruptive.

8. The focal point for loyalty

Finally, in most small churches, the primary focal point of the members' institutional commitment is directed more clearly at the congregation as a whole rather than toward the components. In larger churches, many of the members' primary loyalty is directed toward the minister, while others' basic loyalty is to an adult Sunday school, to the women's organization, to the youth program, to an administrative committee, or to some other subgroup or subcommittee within that large congregation. The stronger the members' basic identification with that congregation as a whole, rather than with a smaller subgroup, the stronger the institutional fabric of the church.

In summary, several of the characteristics that set the small-membership church apart from larger congregations are also factors behind its institutional resilience.

C. What Will Be the Impact of the Urban-to-Rural Migration?

From 1820 to the mid-1960s (with the exception of a five-year period in the 1930s during the Great Depression), the basic population migration in the United States has been from rural to urban areas. A long-term reversal of this pattern began during the mid- to late 1960s. The dominant

---

*It also must be added that the stronger the role of the laity, the less likely a congregation will experience a continuing pattern of numerical growth.

migration pattern in the United States (and in most parts of Canada) today is from urban to rural communities.

Between 1970 and 1980, for example, nonmetropolitan counties in the United States experienced a population increase of 15.4 percent, compared to a 9.1 percent increase for all the metropolitan counties. For the 1975-79 period, for each five people who moved from a nonmetropolitan county into a metropolitan county, seven moved in the other direction from a metropolitan county to a nonmetropolitan county.

There are many reasons for this new migration pattern. One obvious one is the price of urban land. Another is the desire of many employers to relocate to a smaller community where both land costs and labor costs will be less. Equally significant are the growing disenchantment with the urban environment, the fear of crime, the desire for a more relational basis for life, and the widespread perception of the attractiveness of the amenities of rural life. Certainly a major factor is the gradual maturing of the American population and the longer life expectancies of recently retired persons.

It should be noted that the use of the census category of "Standard Metropolitan Statistical Areas" (SMSA) conceals part of the magnitude of this trend, since many predominantly rural counties are now included as part of a metropolitan area. An example of this is Collin County, Texas. It is identified by the Census Bureau as part of the Dallas-Fort Worth metroplex, but it is still largely a rural and small-town county. The population more than doubled— from 67,000 in 1970 to 144,000 in 1980—but it is not an urban community. Many of the newcomers came there to enjoy the benefits of country living while they commute to Dallas for a city paycheck. The residents of Collin County are a part of the 95 million Americans who live in small-town and rural America. This includes the 10,000 residents of McKinney, the largest city in Collin County.

1. A new potential for growth

Collin County represents the first and most obvious of the many ramifications of this new trend that will affect tens of thousands of small churches. While it is impossible to predict all the consequences and implications of the urban-to-rural migration, it is possible to identify several. The first of these is a change in the community context and in the potential for growth in many small-town and rural congregations. Scores of churches in Collin County, Texas, already are experiencing that change. In the past, the popular stereotype was of urban churches growing in numbers and size while rural congregations were shrinking as a result of the population exodus.

The factual basis for that excessively simplistic stereotype has changed. During the 1970-80 decade, more counties registered an increase in population than in any previous decade. During the 1970s, a total of 2,554 counties had an increase in population, compared to the previous record of 2,348 during the 1890-1900 decade. Only 579 counties reported a net loss of population during the 1970s.

As a result of this redistribution of population growth, many small-town and rural churches now have an enhanced potential for numerical growth. This is one reason behind the sudden surge of interest in developing strategies for numerical growth in small-membership churches. Literally tens of thousands of small-membership congregations in small-town and rural America now are faced with the opportunity for significant numerical growth.

2. A demand for new church development

This leads to the second of the many consequences of this new pattern of population migration. During the 1920s, and again during the 1950s and 1960s, new church development was concentrated largely in the larger central cities and in their suburbs. For the last third of this century, the most fertile areas for new church development will be in places such as Collin County, Texas, and a thousand other counties that are experiencing this urban-to-rural migration.

Some of the results of that will be predictably divisive. Already one can hear statements such as these, "Why should anyone want to start new churches out here when we already have plenty?" "Instead of starting new churches, why don't they give the long-established congregations a chance to reach and serve these newcomers?" "How come that new church out on the edge of town is already larger than we are, and we've been here for over sixty years?" "I don't object to organizing new churches, but why does our denominational leadership expect us to help pay for them? That's asking us to subsidize our own competition." "This community has doubled in population in less than ten years, but our congregation hasn't grown at all. Maybe we need a new pastor who is more aggressive in reaching the new people."

In general, new congregations tend to be more likely than long-established churches to reach newcomers, to attract younger adults, to be responsive to the needs of people with no active church relationship, and to develop innovative programs. These characteristics tend to exacerbate the differences between the oldtimers and the newcomers in a growing community.

3. A new community context

A third, and far more subtle consequence of the urban-to-rural migration is an inevitable change in the context of ministry. Most small-town and rural churches operate in a community setting that is very supportive of the church. Frequently that begins to change with the arrival of a large number of "strangers."

In many rural and small-town communities, there is a long history of a very supportive attitude toward the churches. The churches are among the most important institutions in the community. If the minister accepts it, the role of pastor carries with it considerable status as an influential community leader. The departure of a pastor or the arrival of a new minister is a significant event in the lives of many people, including some who are not members of that congregation. A similar, very supportive, attitude of the general community toward the churches also can be seen in many urban neighborhoods where there is a strong nationality, ethnic, racial, or language basis for the homogeneity of the residents of the neighborhoods, and where the churches reflect that ethnic homogeneity. An example of this supportive community attitude can be found in one "hill country" town in south Texas. Most of today's residents are members of one of the several German Lutheran or German Catholic congregations, but there is a strongly supportive community attitude displayed toward the United Methodist and the United Church of Christ congregations in that town. The loyalty of the residents to the Catholic and Lutheran parishes provides a supportive context for all churches.

At the other end of this spectrum is the hostile context found in many inner-city neighborhoods, where some of the churches are viewed by residents as alien institutions maintained largely for the benefit of the ex-residents who drive back in for worship and meetings. When the membership of the churches no longer reflects the ethnic, racial, social class, language, or nationality background of the residents of the community, it is not unusual for the community context to change from supportive, to neutral, to hostile. In some cities, the evidences of this hostile community context can be seen in frequent acts of vandalism, locked doors with peepholes, fenced and guarded parking lots, high insurance rates, and arson.

Somewhere between these two points on the scale are the growing number of communities where the churches are largely ignored. There is a marked absence of either support or hostility. A fairly common example is the resort community where church attendance may drop (because many of the members have to work all day Sunday) when the tourist season is at its peak. The churches ignore the visitors and the visitors ignore the churches.

Just to the supportive side of the middle of the spectrum is the new subdivision where the developer reserves two good sites for churches in the preliminary plot, but expects to be paid $100,000 to $300,000 or more for each parcel of land. On the other side of the center is the community in which the land developer refuses to sell land for a church site, or where deed restrictions prohibit the construction of a church building.

In hundreds of communities, the new migration is changing the context for ministry from supportive to neutral, or even to hostile.

To some extent it is possible to forecast the probable impact on a particular congregation by asking four diagnostic questions.

First, do most of the newcomers moving to this community already have friends, relatives and/or fellow employees living here? If the answer is yes, that reduces the role of the church as a place where newcomers meet and make new friends. If the majority of newcomers do not have friends and relatives already living here, this often means a larger role for the churches as a place newcomers can meet new friends, gain a sense of belonging, feel they are welcomed and needed, and put down their roots. One of the largest business corporations on the continent, which also is concerned about the impact on families when employees are transferred from one job to a new job in another community, urges its employees to join a church as soon as possible after moving to a new location. This advice is offered on the premise that the churches, more than any other community groups, are open, receptive, prepared to welcome and assimilate newcomers and to help them gain a sense of community.

The second question concerning newcomers is, Do the people now living here and the newcomers tend to have an above-average level of competence and experience in building relationships with strangers? If the answer is yes, this may mean that the churches can assume that the residents, both new and old, will take a part of the initiative required to seek out a new church home and to become a part of that worshiping community. In other words, the churches may take a more passive stance in responding to these newcomers, who often will visit a church before that congregation gets around to visiting the newcomers. In these situations the church callers may be kept busy simply returning the visits of persons who came to the church last Sunday.

If the answer is no, the newcomers to this community do not possess an above-average ability in taking the initiative in building relationships with strangers, the church leaders have two basic choices. One is the passive response summarized in the frequently heard comment, "I can't understand why our church hasn't grown more. There's been a thirty percent increase in the population here during the past several years, but our congregation is no larger than it was ten years ago."

The alternative is for members of that congregation to take the initiative in building relationships with the newcomers through visitation-evangelism calls, direct-mail advertising, special ministries and programs designed to meet the needs of the newcomers, and the expansion of the total program and schedule to enable that congregation to serve more people.

Do the majority of the residents of your community already have friends here or are they seeking new friends? Do the residents of your community have an above-average level of competence in building relationships with strangers? Or does the primary responsibility rest on the members of your congregation to build relationships with the residents who are not active in the life of any worshiping congregation?

The third facet of this issue is expressed by the question, How do you view the newcomers? Many church leaders assume that all newcomers will seek out a church on their own initiative if they are committed Christians, and they will remain within the same denominational family.

By contrast, there is a growing body of research evidence that suggests (a) when people change their place of residence they have a tendency to drop out of church if it is now impossible to "go back home to church" because of distance, (b) when people move to a new residence they are more open to a change of denominational affiliation, (c) new residents tend to be upwardly mobile and (d) upwardly mobile people have a greater-than-average tendency to change denominations.

What are your assumptions about the newcomers to your community? Do you assume a strong sense of denominational loyalty? Do you assume the initiative to develop a new church relationship rests with the newcomers? Do you assume that self-identified Christians will immediately seek out a new church home?

Fourth, is this a community in which newcomers and oldtimers see one another frequently during the week? Or is this a community in which many of the residents leave to go to work and rarely see other residents during the week?

In "bedroom communities" where large numbers of people commute to work, the churches must carry a greater burden in helping people become better acquainted. This fact of life should be taken into account in the design of a new building or in a remodeling project, in planning offstreet parking facilities, in allocating the amount of time between the close of the Sunday school hour and the beginning of the worship experience, in the number and variety of fellowship events that are scheduled each year, and in the procedures for the assimilation of new members. These churches have to structure in socializing opportunities for the members.

How often do the members of your congregation see one another between Sundays? Has that pattern changed during the past dozen years? Are there different answers to that question for newcomers and for long-time residents? For men and for women? How have you compensated for this in program development and in planning for building facilities?

The response to this change in the community context may be a very influential factor in determining whether a particular small-town or rural congregation will grow in size as the population grows.

4. *The conflicting expectations*

A fourth product of this urban-to-rural migration can be illustrated by this statement from a new member of a 130-member congregation in a small town in Pennsylvania. "My husband and I were both reared in big churches. We've always looked forward to the day when we could move to a small town and join a small church like this one. We love the informality, the friendliness, the spontaneous way that people care for one another and the deep feeling of fellowship. We think it's great the way everyone can call everybody else by name. How come you don't have the kind of program for our two teenagers that they had in the church we just left?''

To understand that statement, and some related reactions of newcomers, it may be helpful to back off and look at a larger picture.

In broad general terms, many large churches resemble, in anthropological terms, a tribe. The tribe is composed of individuals, families, clans, and other groups with a long-established hierarchy of leaders. It also is large enough to provide a variety of services to the members.

By contrast, the small-town church often resembles a clan composed of a few families, while many really small rural churches resemble a family.

The person moving from a tribe to a clan or a family appreciates the friendliness, the intimacy, the spontaneity of caring and the relational dimensions of the clan—but may not recognize that the trade-off is a reduction in program that is less than the tribal level of services.

The person who was a tribal leader feels a sense of being demoted in being asked to begin as a worker in a clan—where many leadership roles are filled on the basis of good bloodlines rather than competence or past experience.

The minister who grew up in a tribe, or served as the "assistant medicine man" in a tribe following graduation from seminary, may have adjustment problems after becoming the pastor in a clan or a family. That move requires developing a new model for ministry.

The active lay leader, who brings a very "business-like" approach to church affairs after years of service as an officer in a tribe, may experience considerable culture shock on seeing how the business of the clan or family is conducted.

In summary, our religious institutions have assumed that

the basic migration pattern is rural-to-urban and clan-to-tribe. We have had very little experience in developing concepts to understand, or skills to facilitate, the adjustment involved in the urban-to-rural or the tribe-to-clan migration. (The major tension is in the tribe-to-clan migration. The very small family churches tend not to attract newcomers, so we have had much less experience with that type of adjustment.)

5. *The increasing number of night owls*

Finally, there is one other dimension of contemporary society that must be related to the urban-to-rural migration. This is the rapid increase in the number of people working night shifts. Excluding those who work rotating shifts, there are approximately twelve million Amricans who work nights. They range from security people, computer operators, employees in the all-night grocery, hospital staff, night school teachers, to assembly line employees. Perhaps one fifth of them also have a regular daytime job.

A disproportionately large number of the night-shift workers reside outside the larger urban centers and commute to work. Hundreds of small-town churches have discovered their schedules are designed for people who work days. In order to expand their outreach they have added a 4 P.M. Sunday, 6 P.M. Saturday, or 7 P.M. Thursday worship service. A few have adjusted the time of meeting for committees and councils or boards in order to include members who work nights. For the most part, however, Protestant congregations are administered by people who work days, and thus the schedule usually is designed for the convenience of people who work the day shift.

D. What Is Unique About the Multi-Church Parish?

Any discussion of the small-membership chuch would be incomplete if it did not include reference to the multi-church charge or parish. There are at least 60,000 Protestant congregations in the United States and Canada that share a pastor with one or more other churches. This is an especially common practice in The United Methodist Church, the Lutheran Church in America, and a half-dozen denominations; although, as was pointed out in chapter 3, the dominant trend is away from the practice and toward the part-time minister who serves only one congregation. Two out of five United Methodist congregations are linked in circuits in which one minister serves two churches, and one out of five is part of a circuit that includes three or more churches.

There are at least a half-dozen perspectives that can be useful in reviewing the unique characteristics of the congregation that shares a minister with another church.

1. *The peak hour*

The most obvious is the "peak hour problem" on Sunday morning. While there are obvious values in each church's being able to have a regularly scheduled worship at the same hour every Sunday morning, this has its costs. Perhaps the most obvious is that the minister is deprived of the most useful minutes of the entire week for the pastoral care of the members—the few minutes as people gather for worship and the half hour following the benediction.

In the long run, the most serious cost is that the pastor's teaching ministry is sharply limited because of the need to share Sunday morning with another congregation. This is especially significant in those churches with a very strong Sunday school tradition. The research evidence suggests very strongly a close relationship between the strong Sunday school and the pastor's regularly teaching a class in the Sunday school.

In those arrangements in which the minister preaches in

three different churches every Sunday morning, the peak hour squeeze is even more acute. A common result is the reduction of each worship service to forty or fifty minutes in length.

What can be done to reduce the pressure of the peak hour problem? Perhaps the most widely used response is to train a cadre of lay persons to begin and conduct the worship service at the appointed time. The minister arrives after the beginning of the service and usually arrives in time to offer the pastoral prayer, preach the sermon and share in the leadership of the last thirty minutes or so of the service.

A growing response is a product of the recent increase in the number of clergy couples. Both are ordained. Each one wants to serve as a pastor, but each is willing to serve on less than a full-time salary. A frequent pattern is for this couple to serve as the ministerial team for a two- or three-church parish. From the congregation's perspective, this often is the best answer. The congregations have the benefit of two ministers' time, but do not have to provide two parsonages or two salaries. One disadvantage is there is still a comparative scarcity of clergy couples. Another is, as one wife commented, "Shop talk squeezes out the time for pillow talk." In some situations, the gifts and competence of the wife clearly outshine the gifts and talents of the husband, and that can create problems in what is still a male-dominated society where the typical male ego is not as strong as the female ego.

Another response to the peak hour pressure is for one minister to serve as the full-time pastor for two to four congregations with the assistance of a person who shares the responsibility for Sunday morning. This person might be a college student preparing for the ministry, a retired minister, a seminary graduate who is a homemaker or in secular employment rather than in the professional ministry and is available for regular preaching responsibilities, a trained lay preacher, a seminary intern, a chaplain, or a teacher. The ordained minister with one or two such limited-time assistants can serve as the pastor for three congregations, teach in the Sunday church school at one of them and preach in each church every third Sunday. From an economic perspective this may be the most efficient method of providing full-time ministerial leadership for small-membership churches.

2. Who is Number Two?

A second perspective to use in reviewing the unique characteristics of the multi-church parish is psychological. In most two-church charges one congregation is widely perceived as "the big church" and the other is seen as the "second-class operation." One congregation pays the larger share of the salary, one gets first choice for the best hour for Sunday morning worship and receives a larger share of the minister's time, creativity, energy, and loyalty. The second adjusts to the needs and desires of the larger congregation. As a Canadian layman from the smaller of the two congregations in a two-church charge once said, "We feel like we're Canada and they act like they're the United States."

There have been hundreds of attempts to overcome this by yoking together two congregations that are nearly equal in size with the understanding that each is responsible for one half of the total compensation of the minister. In some cases, congregations have pursued the quest for equality so far that they rotate the Sunday morning schedule every quarter or once a year.

What is the result?

A frequent result, according to the pastors serving in these arrangements, is that "one congregation expects 60 percent of my time and energy, the other expects 60 percent of my time and energy, each feels it is subsidizing the other and no one is happy."

The experiences of ministers serving two congregations suggest there are many advantages when the larger is at least twice the size of the smaller. In these arrangements, everyone understands the pecking order. Everyone understands why one congregation has the choice hour on Sunday morning, why that church provides two thirds or more of the compensation, why the minister lives in that particular community and why the minister's spouse is move involved in one congregation and largely ignores the other.

3. What do they have in common?

The third perspective for looking at multi-church charges goes back to why they originally were yoked together. An examination of scores of two-church parishes suggests these are the most influential conditions they share in common:

1. It is assumed neither can afford and/or justify a full-time resident minister.

2. They have the same denominational affiliation.

3. It is assumed their combined economic resources will enable the two congregations to provide adequate com pensation for one minister.

4. The meeting places are reasonably close to each other.

5. Neither can find any other congregation with which it could be yoked.

Largely left out of the negotiations are such variables as the theological stance of the congregation, similarities or differences in program, and the type or style of congregational life.

A review of the experiences of scores of two church

parishes suggests that the pastor can be happier and more effective, there will be fewer tension points between the two congregations (and one result of that will be a longer pastorate) if these variables are given more weight in creating the two-church parish:

1. The two congregations are very similar in their theological stance, in their actual system of church government, and in the style of congregational life.

2. One congregation is at least twice the size of the other.

3. The buildings are located in what are obviously separate communities.

4. The buildings are at least eight or ten miles apart.

5. One congregation holds title to the parsonage and is completely responsible for maintaining that building, rather than there being a shared responsibility between the two congregations.

6. The pastor's spouse is an active member of one congregation, but only an occasional visitor at the other church.

7. There is a minimum emphasis on joint programming by the two congregations in the two-church parish. For predictable and natural reasons, the clergy usually are greatly interested in and strongly supportive of joint ventures in programming (one Thanksgiving service, joint Lenten services, or one vacation Bible school) and most of the laity are not interested in attending these joint efforts if they are held at "their church" rather than at "our church."

8. Most important of all, the leaders in the two congregations took the initiative in creating the arrangement and each chose the other church as its partner. This is in contrast to an arrangement initiated by denominational leaders.

4. *The use of discretionary time*

In most two-church parishes, there is a basic workload for the minister in each church. This includes preaching and teaching, administration, pastoral care, and some community leadership. This package normally adds up to twenty to thirty hours of required time in the average week, but it leaves another thirty to forty hours of discretionary time in that average week.

Some of the most effective pastors of two-church parishes will "specialize" in one of the two churches for eight to fifteen months and spend most of that discretionary time with that congregation. This time may be spent on visitation, on expanding the Sunday school, on a building program, on evangelism, or on some other facet of congregational life. After that assignment has been completed, and by that time many of the overworked lay volunteers are ready for some R & R, the minister turns to the other congregation and allocates the larger share of that discretionary time to helping that church expand its ministry.

It should be recognized that some pastors of two-charge parishes use this discretionary time as a community leader, in securing a doctor of ministry degree, in fishing, or in part-time employment, but this usually has little impact on congregational life or on expanding the ministry of either church.

This use of the minister's discretionary time is an important issue for the two-church parish.

5. What is the time frame?

A related item that sets the two- or three-church parish apart from other churches is the length of the time frame for planning.

While it is true the time frame for planning in small-membership churches tends to be shorter than in larger congregations, the two- or three-church parish should be an exception to that generalization. Many pastors have commented over and over that both the minister and the congregations need to think in blocks of time of several months, perhaps eight to sixteen months, in their planning and scheduling. If this is not done, the result often is conflict, tension and misunderstanding that could have been avoided.

6. *The problem of visibility*

Finally, the minister of the two- or three-church parish has to recognize that a normal paranoid assumption is, "If we don't see our minister, that means we're being neglected, and the other church is getting more of our pastor's time than they are entitled to have." This is an almost universal condition.

One response is to schedule, announce *and keep* regular office hours one or two days a week at "the other church." This time can be used for congregational work, counseling, sermon preparation, meetings, and ad hoc visits.

Scores of pastors who serve a church in town where they live, and a congregation meeting in a building in the open country, will always park their car where it is easily visible from the highway when they call on parishioners or while they are at that building during the week.

Others make regular public references to "When I was out here Tuesday afternoon I. . . ."

While the stereotype that the minister works only one day a week is widespread, it is an unusually serious problem for many pastors serving a two-church parish.

E. What About Money-Raising Events?

"We used to have a bazaar every year to raise money for missions, and that was the high point of the year for our women," explained a long-time member of St. Luke's Church, "but a few years ago the church council adopted a rule banning all money-raising activities, so we've dropped the bazaar."

"Let's review this list," suggested an adult counselor to a dozen high-school-age young people at Trinity Church. "You've listed these as the components of the youth program here at Trinity Church: Sunday school, the youth fellowship, retreats, youth choir, car washes and other fund-raising events, parties, church camp, trips, inter-church youth rallies, the softball team, helping with the vacation church school for younger children, and confirmation classes. That's an even dozen. Now, if we had to eliminate eight of these, which four would you keep as the most important to you?"

After considerable discussion, the four that received the most support were the youth fellowship, retreats, trips, and the variety of fund-raising activities which the teenagers conducted regularly to raise money to finance their trips, rallies, parties, and mission projects. When pressed about why they gave such a high priority to fund-raising events, the young people gave a variety of responses. "A lot of kids come to these who don't come to most of our other activities." "They make it possible for us to do things that some kids couldn't participate in if we didn't raise our own money." "That's when new kids really get to be a part of the group." "They keep us from having to be dependent on the church to finance our own program." "That's the only way we could put $300 into a mission project every year. We could never raise that much for missions from dues or collections."

"Our pastor was a contractor before he went to seminary," explained one of the leaders of the 130-member Mt. Horeb Church. "We had talked about the need for a fellowship hall and kitchen for at least twenty years, but everyone knew that was too much for a small church like us. Less than a year after our new minister came, he had convinced us that there would never be a better time to start than now. We did almost all the work ourselves, and the women have raised more than $17,000 from their second-hand shop and from dinners. Without their help we never could have paid for it, and we probably wouldn't have had the courage to start."

These three conversations illustrate one of the most divisive debates that continues in thousands of churches all across the North American continent. Should we approve money-raising projects or should we finance all church programs out of the offering plate? This is a debate that has especially serious implications for small-membership churches and for denominational policies affecting small congregations.

1. Three levels of debate

This discussion usually is conducted on three different levels or from three different perspectives. The first, and the one that usually is articulated most forcefully, is that every congregation should pay its own way, that it should not depend on "outsiders" to help finance someone else's church through purchasing the goods or services sold by that church; that the members should tithe, and therefore the church need not be dependent on dinners, bazaars, car washes, and other fund-raising activities; that the time and energy of the members should be devoted to the ministry, mission, and service programs, rather than wasted on money-raising activities; and that a tax-exempt organization should not compete with tax-paying businesses that sell similar goods and services.

These arguments are usually offered by those who look at this and other subjects from a rational, idealistic, professional, and functional perspective and identify how committed Christians should act.

The second level of the debate over money-raising activities usually is offered by those who look at this and other subjects from a pragmatic, relational, behavioristic, and organizational perspective. Among the arguments offered by this group are ones similar to why the high school students placed fund-raising activities among their top four priorities. A closely related point is that many small-membership churches never would undertake large-scale mission projects, construction programs, or outreach ministries, unless the members had the reassurance of a fund-raising event to help finance those ventures.

Leaders concerned with strengthening the organizational life of the congregation often point out that an annual fund-raising project is the specific, attainable, measurable, visible, rewarding, and unifying goal that helps unify the women's organization, the men's group, or the adult Sunday school. They add that these projects also offer an unparalleled "entry point" for new members to come into a group, to get acquainted, to be "initiated into the tribe" and to feel needed. Others point out that fund-raising activities offer opportunities for individuals who do not feel competent—to teach a class, to function as a committee member, to counsel a youth group, to make visitation-evangelism calls, or to lead a worship experience to make a contribution of their time and energy and to express their commitment through participation in one of these money-making projects. These activities also provide a neutral, nonthreatening, and enjoyable opportunity for constituents, prospective new members, and other unchurched people to meet members of the congregation and to become acquainted with the church. Some proponents of this perspective also contend that a distinctive money-raising project helps to reinforce the unique identity of each group, organization, circle, class, or fellowship within that congregation. Others point out that these activities offer members the opportunity to express their nonverbal skills, to share in memorable experiences, to help build a sense of togetherness and reinforce the group spirit; that they provide some members with a sense of worth and being needed, foster the cooperative spirit, and serve as a "probationary" experience for future leaders.

Leaders from blue-collar congregations, black churches, and Hispanic churches argue that the ban on money-raising events is simply another attempt by upper-middle-class-white church leaders to impose their standards and values on others.

The third level of the debate usually receives the least attention and is concerned with the "trade-offs" of the subject. How can a congregation secure the advantages of money-raising projects and minimize the disadvantages?

An example of this is the youth group that is organized around a major emphasis on events, experiences, trips, and other expensive components such as a work camp experience. If the whole program is financed out of the regular church budget, it usually produces many complaints about the high cost of the youth ministry (typically $100 to $500 per young person) and may create an unhealthy dependency among the young people. If each young person is expected to pay the full cost through a special assessment of the costs, this will exclude many teenagers and lower the participation rate. If the young people are prohibited from engaging in money-raising projects, that approach is eliminated from youth ministries. Sometimes a heavy emphasis on fund-raising activities, such as are involved in financing a two-week youth choir trip, means that these money-raising events become the largest part of the total youth program, and this discourages those teenagers who will not be able to take advantage of the trip.

Frequently the discussion on the trade-offs can be the

most productive level of the debate on this subject, but too often it is largely ignored.

2. Six alternatives

What do other congregations do about this subject? While no exhaustive answer is available to this question, most of the responses can be placed in one of six categories.

The first is the easiest to describe. All fund-raising activities are strictly prohibited!

The second consists of two safeguards. A limit is placed on the number of fund-raising events that are permitted. This may be one per year for all groups and organizations combined. In general, the larger the congregation, the higher the ceiling. The other safeguard is that the money raised by any *adult* event or activity *must* be given away and cannot be used to meet any local budget needs. (Occasionally an exception is made for a building program or for some other capital expenditure, as well as for youth activities.)

A third response is the one, big, congregation-wide, annual fund-raising event, such as a dinner or a bazaar, in which all classes, groups, circles and other organizations are invited to participate. Sometimes the proceeds are earmarked in advance for a specific cause, and sometimes the money is divided among the participating organizations and each can allocate it as the members of that group decide, but there is only one money-raising event per year in that congregation. This course of action is chosen by many small-membership congregations in order to avoid overworking their small loyal core of members and to reduce the possibility that money-raising events will dominate the life of the congregation.

A fourth response is to place a time limit on these events. For example, in one congregation no event can be held for more than two successive years. In another, each group, class, organization, or circle is permitted only one money-raising event per year. There is a ceiling on the number of events in order to prevent these fund-raising activities from becoming the heart of the program for any group, but there are no restrictions on the allocation of the funds.

The fifth response is when there is no congregationally imposed limitation on money-raising activities.

The sixth, but perhaps least common, response is when a congregation or denomination has some type of money-raising event or solicitation of funds intentionally planned to invite non-member support of that church's missionary program. The annual "Ingathering" of the Seventh-day Adventists is an example of this.

3. Three caution signs

Finally, it may be helpful to raise three caution signs. First, if and when money-raising events are banned, this prohibition should be preceded by this question, "What will we replace these activities with that will offer attractive 'entry points' for newcomers, that will provide for a nonverbal expression of the individual's commitment, that will produce an equivalent sacrificial response by our members, and that also will have the characteristics of a specific, attainable, measurable, visible, rewarding, and unifying goal?"

The second caution is that many of the proposed replacements for money-raising activities tend to produce a disappointing response because they are not accompanied by an adequate lay-training program that both enhances the competence and reinforces the self-confidence of the participants. By contrast, fund-raising activities are often based on skills and abilities already possessed by many members.

The third warning is a direct challenge to a large body of

conventional wisdom and a range of denominational practices.

Many denominations that discourage or ban money-raising activities allocate millions of dollars every year in direct and indirect subsidies to small-membership churches. From this observer's experience, it appears that denominational subsidies tend to produce dependency, passivity, low morale, and self-centeredness. They tend to undercut the level of congregational esteem. Subsidized congregations tend to have a weak sense of mission and outreach beyond the membership. Frequently the leaders devote an excessive amount of time and energy to their efforts to perpetuate that subsidy from the denomination. Long-established congregations that have a long history of receiving financial subsidies from denominational sources rarely turn out to be numerically growing churches.

By contrast, money-raising activities tend to reinforce a sense of mission and outreach.* They tend to foster a sense of self-sufficiency and independence. These activities combat passivity and often produce a sense of activity, excitement, involvement, progress, and future orientation.

Which do you favor? Denominational subsidies for small-membership churches or removing the ban on money-raising activities?

F. Enabler or Leader?

One of the most critical policy questions concerning the future of the small church concerns the leadership role** of the pastor.

---

*In most denominations, there is a long history of the missionary program's being heavily dependent on congregationally sponsored money-raising events and activities.

**It should be emphasized that the issue being raised here is not one of personalities or of *styles* of ministerial leadership. The issue focuses on the leadership *role* of the minister and the pastor's ability and willingness to be

The Small Church Is Different!

For the past thirty years there has been a growing body of thought that suggests that the ideal leadership role for the pastor is to be an enabler or facilitator who causes the laity to identify and carry out their ministry.

This concept has much to commend it. The fourth chapter of Paul's letter to the Ephesians is one of the most frequently cited foundations for this concept. What is often overlooked, however, is that this is the most demanding leadership role a minister can assume.[11] The effective enabler is a remarkably gifted individual who has mastered a wide range of skills and is willing to work long hours, day after day, and week after week. This role also requires an immense amount of patience. Very few theological seminaries are equipped to teach the range of skills required of the effective enabler.

The hard-working and highly skilled enabler can often facilitate remarkable changes in the life, the spiritual journey, and the personal growth of individuals—but usually that means a long tenure of at least seven to ten years or more in a congregation of fewer than 200 members. There is a severe shortage of highly skilled, hard-working and patient enablers who are willing to serve a small-membership church for that long!

The practical parish experience with this leadership role suggests very strongly that the most common products of today's self-styled enablers are (a) congregations that do not grow, (b) charges by the laity that the minister is incompetent or lazy, and/or (c) passivity, as the members wait for the minister to lead, and the minister is attempting to "out-passive" the congregation.

Experience suggests that the usual expression of the enabler role is inappropriate for the congregation averaging more than 100 to 150 at worship, the congregation

an initiating or active leader rather than a passive reactor to the initiative of others and to external forces.

experiencing rapid numerical growth, or pastorates lasting less than seven to ten years.

Seminary professors and denominational leaders need to rethink this whole issue—or recognize they are encouraging a role that will limit the potential growth of thousands of small-membership churches.

There also is the very practical question of whether denominational leaders can afford to endorse a course of action that (a) is incompatible with numerical church growth, (b) means starting new congregations instead of expecting existing churches to reach the newcomers, particularly in those communities that are growing as a result of the urban-to-rural migration, (c) may require long term direct and/or indirect financial subsidies for self-styled enablers serving small churches, and (d) may result in a decrease in the size of the membership and the outreach of that denomination.

G. What About the Organizational Structure?

One of the central theses of this book is that the small church is not a small-scale version of the large congregation and that denominational and ministerial policies and priorities should be tailored to fit the unique characteristics of the small church. The small-membership church is different! One of the most important applications of this concept is in the system of governance.

To oversimplify a complex issue, small-membership churches can be divided into three categories.

The smallest of these is the "fellowship," the long-established congregation with less than 35 or 40 at worship. These congregations often function as overgrown small groups and have a very informal decision-making process with a minimum of committee or board meetings. Frequently the most meaningful policy questions are not resolved at an official meeting, but rather in someone's home or some other informal gathering. These congregations require very little administrative structure.

The next category is the congregation averaging between 35 to 90 at the principal weekly worship service. The system of church governance in these congregations usually (a) places a modest load on standing committees; (b) assumes the governing body will not only make major policy decisions, but also spend considerable time and energy on details that in larger congregations are resolved by committees; (c) expects individuals, many of whom are on the governing board, to carry the followup responsibility on matters that in larger churches would be delegated to a committee; (d) causes people to accept the fact that several times a year the monthly meeting of the governing board will last for three hours or longer because of the details that must be discussed by that body; (e) places great weight on the value of participatory democracy and relies on the members at a congregational meeting to be the point of final authority when a major policy issue has to be decided; (f) has modest expectations of the pastor as an initiating leader or as a power figure; (g) operates on a more or less informal basis; and (h) expects the governing body, and possibly the Christian education committee, to be the major sources of creativity and innovation in programming and outreach.

This is an acceptable system for most stable congregations in this size bracket. If the leaders expect these churches to grow in size, however, it usually will mean (a) a change in that system of church governance, (b) overloading the members of the governing body, (c) slowing the pace of decision making, or (d) producing an excessive amount of frustration over the failure to agree on priorities in the allocation of scarce resources.

The third of these three approaches to church governance is the one appropriate for those congregations that are stable in size and are in the bracket of perhaps 85 to 150 at worship on Sunday morning, *and for the somewhat smaller congregations with an aggressive and systematic new-member recruitment system.*

In these congregations, the system of governance usually (a) places heavy expectations on both administrative and program committees, such as Christian education, worship, evangelism, finance, property, pastoral relations, and missions, (b) assumes the governing body will focus on broad policy questions as it trusts the judgment and affirms the recommendations of committees, (c) assigns those agenda items to be delegated to committees rather than to individuals who also are members of the board, (d) schedules the governing body to meet for 90 to 150 minutes at the regular monthly meeting with few special meetings of that body, and only rarely do the board meetings last for more than two-and-one half hours, (e) functions as a representative democracy and assumes that for almost all issues the governing body is the actual point of final appeal—and only rarely are divisive issues brought up at heavily attended congregational meetings, (f) expects the pastor to be a strong initiating leader, (g) operates on a less informal and a more "business-like" model of administration, and (h) expects creativity and innovation in programming and outreach to originate in the committee structure and from the pastor, rather than from the governing body.

The distinction in the appropriate system of governance among congregations of different size (and complexity) is one of the most commonly neglected subjects when the discussion is on either church polity or on church growth.

H. Should We Cooperate?

One of the most widely advocated responses to the limitations of resources in small-membership churches is the suggestion that they join with other congregations in cooperative ventures. This is an extremely complex subject and merits book-length treatment, but five observations can be offered here.

1. A fragile concept

The first point that must be made is that most clusters, cooperative ministries, and similar arrangements tend to be very fragile creations. Frequently they are short-lived. Several efforts have been made to study a large group of cooperative ministries. Each of these large-scale studies has found the reputed number of cooperative ministries to exceed the reality. If one were to drive across the country, for every active and healthy cooperative ministry that one would encounter, one would find at least a half dozen corpses, two or three cooperative ministries suffering from severe malnutrition, and one or two that clearly are on the verge of dying.

This is not to suggest that intercongregational cooperation is a bad idea, nor to discourage efforts in this direction. The intent here is far simpler. Cooperative ministries are very fragile institutional expressions of the universal Church. Unless they are handled with care, they tend to break up, fade way, disappear, evaporate, or dissolve. By contrast, the parish church is a very tough ecclesiastical institution and usually can survive rough handling, shocks, disasters, neglect, and abuse that would be fatal to the typical cooperative ministry.

2. Too many "publics"

A second characteristic of most cooperative ministries, and one of the factors behind their institutional fragility, is the accountability to too many "publics" or groups. There are at least five publics or groups of people in the typical congregation. One is composed of the people whom the congregation is *primarily* concerned with serving. A second is composed of the governing board of the congregation. A third is composed of the people who provide the financial support for the congregation. A fourth is composed of the people who provide the personal, moral, and psychological support for the professional staff. The fifth is composed of the people the church or the pastor is trying to influence by what that organization is or does.

In the typical worshiping congregation most of the people in at least four or five of these publics are members of that congregation. This overlapping of the several publics tends to be a unifying force. In the typical cooperative ministry, however, there may be only a very limited overlap among the members of these five publics. It may be trying to serve a group of children and teenagers who do not belong to any church. The board may be composed of members of the congregations that created the cooperative ministry. One half or more of the financial support may come from denominational agencies. The support group for the director may come from three or four pastors. The advocacy ministry is directed at public officials. The separation of these publics creates a major point of vulnerability for cooperative ministries.

3. *The duds and the bombs*

Perhaps the most distinctive characteristic of cooperative ministries, and especially those involving urban congregations, is in the responsibilities assigned the cooperative. This is another reason why they tend to be so fragile. What is the nature of these responsibilities? In plain language they can be described as the duds and the bombs. This point can be illustrated by looking at some examples.

"How many young single adults do you have who are

active in the program of your congregation?" asked Pastor Green of three of his colleagues. "None," responded one. "A couple," replied another. "No more than two or three," said a third. "That's our situation, too, and that's why I asked the question," continued Pastor Green. "Our church simply has not been able to reach the 18 to 24 age group. Why don't we get together and set up a cooperative ministry and see if we can do a better job of reaching that age group through a joint effort?" Each of the four congregations had been unsuccessful in ministering to young single adults, so the decision was made to turn this "dud" over to the new cooperative ministry as its first priority.

"I believe the churches should be heard from on the subject of racial integration and school busing," declared an active layman at the Oak Park Church. "We talked about that at our board meeting the other night," responded a layman from Grace Church, "and nearly everyone there decided that if we tried to take a stand on that explosive issue, it would split our congregation." "That's about where we came out at our council meeting last month," added a layman from Trinity Church. "We decided that it was too hot an issue for our congregation to get into now." "I guess I hear what you're saying," replied the layman from the Oak Park Church. "Maybe the best way to handle it would be by setting up an interchurch agency and have that agency be the Christian voice in this community on these controversial issues." What he was proposing was to form a cooperative ministry and hand it the bombs that were too explosive for individual congregations to handle.

"We used to have a lot of members who lived right in this neighborhood around our church," commented the minister at the Tenth Street Church, "but today we have only a handful who live within a mile of the building. We've tried to reach the newcomers here, but we haven't had any success. I don't know what to do next." "That's our situation, too," declared the pastor from nearby St. Luke's Church. "We have made a neighborhood ministry our top priority ever since I came here four years ago and so far we have had no success whatsoever." "We're in about the same boat," added the minister from Bethel Church. "Why don't we see if we can get four or five of these churches here to form a cooperative ministry and develop a single unified approach to reaching the people in this neighborhood?" Again the proposal was to hand a dud to the yet-to-be-created cooperative ministry.

"As near as I can tell by looking at the records this congregation peaked in size in 1922 or 1923," commented the recently arrived minister who served the 80-member Pine Ridge Church and two other congregations as part of a three-church rural parish. "We celebrated our seventy-fifth anniversary last year, and our church never has had a full-time minister," commented the high school social science teacher who also was the part-time pastor at nearby Bethany Church. "I was talking with two of our leaders the other night," added the 68-year-old retired minister who was the supply preacher at Zion Church, "and they told me they felt our church was dying. Neither one expects that congregation to be in existence ten years from today. They were very frank about it." "My hunch is that all three of these congregations will be gone within a decade," suggested the teacher. "Maybe we should try to bring several of our lay leaders together and try to develop some form of cooperative ministry. Perhaps the future of these and some of the other small rural churches out here lies in cooperation."

Too often, cooperative ministries are launched out of a sense of frustration, powerlessness, fear, or hopelessness and are assigned responsibilities that have proved impossible for the congregations to respond to unilaterally or that are too explosive for any one congregation to cope with by itself. Placing these duds and bombs at the top of the agenda of the cooperative ministry is one means of accentuating the fragility of intercongregational cooperation.

The obvious moral of this is that it may be wise to include at least one or two winners in the responsibilities assigned to a new cooperative ministry.

4. *The seven basic types*

Any proposal for two or more small-membership churches to join together in some form of cooperative ministry will be reinforced if there is widespread agreement on exactly what is being suggested. One way of improving the quality of communication on this subject is to think in terms of the seven basic types of cooperative ministries.

Perhaps the most common type of cooperative ministry is the one designed to provide specific programs from an interchurch base. Under this broad umbrella are two subcategories of this type of cooperative ministry, those whose program is directed primarily at the members of the participating congregations and those whose program is directed primarily at nonmembers.

Three examples of the former are the union Thanksgiving service for members from a three-church parish, the joint teacher training program for five small town churches, and the joint confirmation program. Examples of a cooperative program directed toward nonmembers include the ministry with children from migrant families, the creation of a golden age club for senior citizens, or the "common pantry" to provide emergency food supplies. Most of these cooperative ventures in programming beyond the membership tend to be directed at the very young, the old, or the poor.

A second, but very rare, type of cooperative ministry is the one directed at challenging, enabling, and strengthening the participating congregations. This type usually was created *primarily* to help congregations in transition make the change from one role to a new role, but it has attracted very limited interest and support.

There are at least four reasons for this. First, relatively few congregations that find themselves in what is now an obsolete role seek help. Most focus on survival goals, not on planned change. Second, those congregations that do succeed in identifying a new role, developing a new identity, and adapting to a new day usually decide they need to focus all their resources on this effort and find it uncomfortable, difficult, or impossible to participate as an active member of a cooperative ministry.

Third, there is a widespread assumption that the responsibility for challenging, enabling, and strengthening congregations rests with the staff of the regional judicatory of the denomination or with the national staff, not with a cooperative ministry. For a new venture in interchurch cooperation to be formed for this purpose would appear to many to be intruding on someone else's jurisdiction.

Fourth, most cooperative ministries have a strong built-in bias toward maintaining or perpetuating the status quo and thus this role runs counter to that natural tendency.

There are a number of rural cooperative ministries that have been created to challenge small rural churches to respond to a new era and to help them develop a new role, but these are comparatively rare in urban America. One of the outstanding urban examples is the Churches-in-Transition ministry staffed by Walter Ziegenhals of the Chicago Renewal Society.

This could become the fastest growing area in interchurch cooperation, since this is a means of making available on a continuing basis the services of a professional change agent with skills in counseling with congregations. The ideal arrangement would group the participating churches by type and by community setting, rather than simply by geography and/or denominational label. For example, one venture might be composed of open country churches in some of the thousand nonmetropolitan counties that are showing a net population gain by migration. The focus there might be on helping those congregations become evangelistic churches seeking to reach and to minister to the new residents who want to combine country living with a city paycheck.

Another might be a cooperative ministry composed of the "downtown First Churches" in county-seat communities. A third type might be composed of the rural churches in summer vacation communities. A fourth might be composed of a group of urban ex-neighborhood type congregations. By working together, these churches can secure the services of a skilled parish consultant who would facilitate the development of a new role for each congregation.

A third type of cooperative ministry, and the one that is most widely accepted by small rural churches, is the one that was designed to provide ministerial leadership for the participating churches. The "larger parish" is a very common form of this type of cooperative.

Until recently, there was less interest among urban churches than in rural communities in cooperative staffing arrangements. A very productive example of this type of cooperative arrangement is when several churches share the time of one staff person specializing in leadership development and program building. The most common arrangement is when two congregations call the same individual to serve as the pastor of both churches. A third example is for several congregations to share the cost, and the services, of a full-time resident specialist in Christian education.

Inflationary factors and the rising cost of person-centered services mean this type of cooperative ministry probably will continue to attract attention.

The simplest version of this model is the two-church parish served by one minister. The two congregations operate as autonomous units, except that they share in the calling, compensation, and care of one pastor who serves both congregations.

The fastest growing model of this type of cooperative ministry is the two to five church parish served by a husband-wife ministerial team. The rapid increase in the number of women graduating from theological seminaries has encouraged many husband-wife ministerial teams to look for a cooperative arrangement where two or more congregations will share their professional services.

Back during the 1960s, a substantial number of cooperative ministries were created to fulfill the need for advocates for the poor, the oppressed minorities, and/or to speak to issues. These issue-centered cooperative ministries can act as a very significant safety valve by enabling church members to unite and to act on important, but often highly controversial and frequently very divisive, conflicts within the members' congregations.

While it is unfortunate (in terms of the prophetic responsibilities of the churches), most issue-centered, advocacy types of cooperative ministry have either disappeared because of the drying up of the necessary financial support, or have redefined their role and moved to a different role.

If one reflects on the functions of the church that usually can be carried out most effectively by an interchurch approach, social action and advocacy rank at the top of the list. The declining interest in social action and the prophetic role of the church has resulted in a decrease in the number of this fourth type of intergenerational cooperation.

Occasionally a cooperative ministry is designed to create one or more institutions that will pick up and carry out a specific responsibility. This fifth type of cooperative ministry may take the form of a housing corporation, a private school, a legal aid center, a medical clinic, a lay academy, a nursery school, a social services agency, a camp, or an interchurch center.

For this type of cooperative ministry to be successful, there are two vital requirements. The first is one individual, *not a committee,* who has a clear vision of what must be done, a pressing sense of urgency to turn that vision into reality, and dynamic leadership gifts. The second is a source of financing beyond that provided by the participating congregations or denominations. This might be mortgages insured by the federal government (in the case of a housing corporation), or a foundation (in the case of an interchurch center), tuition (in the case of a private school), a single major benefactor (in the case of a camp), or user fees (in the case of a nursery school).

In addition, this type of cooperative ministry will usually develop its own clientele and support group who often will become more influential in policy formulation than the original founders. This can result in a sharp change in the goals of the institution and thus leave some of the original sponsors with a feeling they have been exploited.

While it has not been an especially effective model, a sixth type of cooperative ministry has been attracting increasing support for the past two decades. This brings several congregations together to develop a common strategy for ministry in a large geographical area. Sometimes this is an interdenominational venture, but more often it is a denominational effort.

There are six major obstacles that repeatedly are encountered by this type of cooperative ministry. The most common is that not all congregations agree on the need and the timing for development of an overall strategy for ministry. Frequently the passive noncooperation of two or three crucial congregations can obstruct an effort by the leaders of several congregations to cooperate on strategy formulation.

A second, and closely related, obstacle is that often the need of a comprehensive strategy is promoted by a few denominational leaders without the necessary "ownership" by pastors and lay leaders.

A third obstacle is that, in many congregations, the gifts, talents, preferences, and value system of the pastor dominate congregational planning. Thus a change of pastors or a vacancy can greatly influence the ideas contributed by a particular congregation in defining its future role as part of an overall strategy. Too often the churches in the area where a comprehensive strategy is desired are also the churches that tend to have a short tenure for ministers.

A fourth problem is that it is difficult, regardless of the abundance of good intentions, to develop an overall strategy unless there has first been a systematic and realistic effort by each of the congregations involved to evaluate its own role, assets, liabilities, potential, and priorities.

A fifth barrier is that frequently there is a difference of expectations among the participants. Some see this as a means of "turning back the calendar" and recreating the past. Others see it as a means of facilitating rapid change. A few may be seeking to promote mergers and church unions, while others are convinced this should be an effort to keep their church from closing or merging. This conflict in expectations may kill the whole effort.

Finally, there usually emerges a major difference of opinion among the participants on the basic priorities for ministry. Until there is widespread agreement on purpose and priorities it usually is difficult to develop a comprehensive strategy that will be acceptable as a guideline for each of the participating congregations.

While it is clearly a different type of venture, one of the

fastest growing segments of interchurch cooperation is the cluster or coalition of congregations that come together to form a cooperative ministry because some of the leaders feel guilty about not cooperating. This guilt is expressed in such phrases as the following. "We should do more together!" "There are so many churches here, maybe we could do more by cooperating." "It's a shame that we all go our own way!" "Everyone else is involved in a cluster, why aren't we doing more in cooperating with other congregations?"

Guilt is not a healthy motivating force for any individual or group, and interchurch cooperation is not an exception. Instead of focusing on the needs of people, on a specific task, or on a clearly defined role, this seventh type of cooperative ministry often exists only on paper, and its central purpose is to ease the guilt of those who formed it. Rarely is it productive!

5. *Church growth or cooperation?*

The last comment on intercongregational cooperation grows out of a growing body of evidence that disturbs many people, including this writer. The evidence suggests that intercongregational cooperation *in programming* and church growth are incompatible. This is an example of a trade-off. We can eat ice cream, *or* we can lose weight, but we cannot do both. The parallel is that the small-membership church may elect to become involved in a cooperative venture in programming with other churches, *or* it may pursue an aggressive new-member recruitment effort. Few churches can do both.

The reasons behind this generalization obviously are speculative, but many of the students of church growth and the proponents of interchurch cooperation agree that intercongregational cooperation rarely results in membership growth in the participating congregations. One reason is that a cooperative ministry may blur the distinctive identity of each participating congregation, and growing churches usually project a clear image of who they are.

Another factor is that, with but few highly visible exceptions, people unite with a specific worshiping congregation, not with a cooperative ministry. Evangelism depends on person-to-person contacts, not on church-to-church relationships.

A third factor is that the people with a strong interest in evangelism and church growth rarely are interested in interchurch cooperation, and vice versa.

A fourth factor is that many cooperative ministries come into existence as the result of the pressures of dwindling resources, and congregations operating from a cut-back motivation rarely attract new members.

Another reason is that interchurch cooperation does use the time and energy of ministers and laity in creating and maintaining a new institution, and that time is not available for membership outreach.

Finally, the history of interchurch cooperation supports the contention that some functions of the church (such as social action, a prophetic witness, maintaining theological seminaries, camps, etc.) can be done most effectively cooperatively. At the other end of the spectrum, some functions of the church can best be carried out unilaterally. That list includes worship, Sunday school, evangelism, and the care of the meeting place. By its failure, the widely publicized interdenominational crusade in evangelism in the early 1970s called Key 73 illustrated that the cooperative production of materials can be carried out effectively, but that evangelism can best be done by individual congregations!

These comments on the incompatibility of church growth and interchurch cooperation should not be interpreted as an argument against cooperative ministries. Instead, these comments have been included here in order to emphasize the value of looking at cooperative ministries by type or category when discussing proposals for new ventures in interchurch cooperation. This can help clarify expectations, goals, and evaluation criteria and avoid frustration and disappointment.

I. Should We Merge?

Back during the 1960-75 era, there was an average of at least three mergers a week that involved two or three Protestant congregations. That also was an era when scores of denominational and ecumenical leaders promoted merger as the best solution to the problems of the small church. During the past several years, there has been a sharp decline in the number of mergers.

People interested in pursuing the merger of two or more small-membership congregations may find it useful to reflect on some of the reasons behind this decline in the urge to merge. Obviously these are somewhat speculative and subjective statements, but they are based on interviews with leaders from more than a score of denominations, as well as on personal observation.

1. Many of the congregational mergers of the 1960s were the product of the denominational mergers of that era. Since nine out of ten local church mergers involve congregations from the same denominational family, it is easy to see why denominational mergers sparked efforts to merge two or three local churches. The merger of 1957 that produced the United Church of Christ, the union of 1958 that created the United Presbyterian Church in the United States of America, the union of 1960 that established The American Lutheran Church, the merger of 1962 that produced the Lutheran Church in America, and the union of 1968 that produced The United Methodist Church caused hundreds of congregations to think about merger. Many of the local

church mergers of that era brought together congregations from two different traditions that were now in the same denomination.

The absence of denominational mergers since 1968 has removed one basic motivation for mergers.

2. Many of the mergers of the 1960-75 era were products of the period's ecumenical enthusiasm. In scores of mergers, the most influential facilitator was a staff member from a council of churches or some other interdenominational agency. The decline of the ecumenical movement and the reduction in the staff of these interdenominational agencies has removed a strong force for merger.

3. During the 1960s there was a widespread interest among church leaders in efficiency and economy. This sparked an interest in encouraging the merger of what appeared to be small and inefficient congregations. The current generation of church leaders displays a greater interest in mission, evangelism, church growth, and outreach. While one generation saw the small congregation as a problem to be "solved," the current generation tends to see the small-membership church as a resource or an asset in mission.

4. Perhaps the most influential factor behind the declining interest in congregational mergers grows out of five lessons from experience.

First, the denominations that displayed the greatest interest in promoting congregational mergers have turned out to be numerically declining denominations.

Second, in too many mergers, the result was 4 plus 4 equals 6. The merger of the 150-member congregation with the 130-member church tended to create a new 200-member congregation, rather than the anticipated 280-member church. In general, the larger the size of the participating congregations, the more disappointing were the results when measured in terms of the resulting membership.

Third, experience suggested that the most successful unions tended to be those that (a) involved three, rather than two congregations, (b) resulted in the creation of a new congregation meeting in a new building at a new location, and (c) were motivated by a strong, future-oriented sense of mission and expanded outreach, rather than by a desire for institutional survival. Few potential mergers meet all three criteria.

Fourth, most mergers were rejected by the participating congregations at least once or twice before eventually being approved. The new generation of literalists among congregational leaders has resulted in many proposed mergers' being rejected when first proposed, and then abandoned when that rejection was assumed to be final. Effective proponents of congregational mergers realize the importance of patience and understand that initial rejection does not mean no! but only no, not at this time.

Finally, the national context has changed. American society has shifted so a lesser value is placed on efficiency, economy, professionalism, and on functional concerns. A greater value is being placed on relationships, on the importance of place, and on one's own personal and spiritual journey. One result of this shift in national values is that the generation of lay leaders who were open and receptive to the idea of congregational mergers is gradually being replaced by a generation that is interested in a substantially different agenda.

Does any of these reasons behind the recent decline in the number of congregational mergers speak to your interest in merger?[12]

J. What Are the Exceptions?

Imagine for a moment that you have been asked to conduct two research projects. The first is to study the characteristics, similarities, and dissimilarities of ten huge congregations, each averaging between 500 and 600 at worship on Sunday morning, and representing ten different denominations.

The second project is to study ten small congregations, each averaging between fifty and sixty at Sunday morning worship, and covering a cross section of churches that size from a single denomination.

What would you discover? One discovery would be that the differences among those ten huge congregations, even though they represent ten different denominations, are fewer and less pronounced than the differences among the ten smaller churches, even though they all are affiliated with the same denomination.

That leads to the last question in this chapter. Are there exceptions to the generalizations that have been offered in these pages? The answer is a resounding yes!

This point can be illustrated by looking briefly at six major exceptions.

The first of these, and perhaps the clearest exception, is the small black congregation. In the typical black church the minister has a far more central role than in the typical white congregation. In addition, the typical black congregation has a more important place in the life of the members, and the organizational life is stronger than in the white counterpart. With the exception of a few denominations, such as the Church of God in Christ, women have a far more influential role in black churches than in white congregations. The typical small black congregation also is more likely to include three or four generations of the same family than is a white church of the same size.

Second, there are many significant differences among small-membership churches from different denominations. In some denominations that operate on the call system for ministerial placement, the pastor of the small church often is placed there following graduation from theological school. This is not uncommon in small rural churches in the Lutheran Church–Missouri Synod, the United Church of Canada, and the Presbyterian Church in Canada.

As was pointed out earlier, the Southern Baptist Convention has several thousand congregations now served by bivocational ministers. By contrast, the Presbyterian Church in the U.S.A. has an extensive program of providing financial subsidies to enable small congregations to have the benefit of a full-time resident minister.

In the typical small church in several denominations, such as the Missionary Church, the Evangelical Covenant Church and the General Association of Regular Baptist Churches, the average attendance at worship usually exceeds the reported membership, and sometimes by a very substantial number.

In The United Methodist Church the small membership congregation is likely to (a) be located in a rural community, (b) share a pastor with one or more other churches, (c) be served by a young pastor coming directly from seminary or by a pastor who has not completed seminary, (d) have a series of very short pastorates, usually four years or less, (e) not be expected by denominational leaders to grow in size, (f) be perceived by many members as a post-seminary apprenticeship for young pastors "on their way up the conference ladder of appointments."

The small United Church of Christ congregation frequently is perceived to be the liberal church in town.

Several denominations, such as the Seventh-day Adventists, the Christian Church (Disciples of Christ), the Cumberland Presbyterian Church, the Advent Christian Church, and the Mennonite Church are very small church denominations.

A third exception is the long-established and heavily endowed small congregation. Most of these are to be found in the northeastern states and in the larger central cities, but there also are many small town churches with large endowments, especially in the Southwest. Typically these congregations receive between $10,000 and $50,000 annually from endowments, bequests, and legacies. This means they often are largely immune from many of the economic pressures that affect the typical small church.

Perhaps the most distinctive exception is the small-membership church composed largely of prosperous and successful farmers and ex-farmers. These members frequently bring a degree of initiative, self-reliance, optimism, creativity, and persistence that often makes these churches immune to the institutional forces at work in most small congregations.

The fifth exception is the recently established small congregation composed entirely of recent immigrants from Korea, Colombia, Samoa, Cuba, Vietnam, Mexico, or some other non-English-speaking part of the world. The ethnic language and immigrant characteristics outweigh most of the points emphasized in this book.

Finally, the small-town church that includes several merchants and community leaders and enjoys the advantages of a long-term pastorate is an exception to much that is written here. [13]

While it may average less than a hundred at worship, and thus be regarded by many as "only a small church," thousands of these congregations have a remarkable degree of vitality, an exceptional interest in missions, and a profound impact on the life of the larger community. Frequently they include a disproportionately large number of very creative and committed leaders (including some farmers who may live five to ten miles out in the country); they offer a broader range of programs, ministries, and activities than does the typical congregation of that size; and they are able to challenge the gifts and skills of some very talented ministers who find these churches to be fulfilling and meaningful places to serve. These are both exceptions to much that is written here, and they are exceptional churches.

Chapter VI

WHAT WILL
TOMORROW BRING?

ost predictions about the future turn out to be wrong. Most predictions about the future tend to err on the side of excessive pessimism. Most predictions about the future reflect past developments rather than new trends.

Those three brief admonitions should cause anyone to be cautious about forecasting the future of such a diverse collection of institutions as small-membership churches. Despite that warning, it appears possible to lift up several trends that will have a profound impact on thousands of small churches during the remainder of the twentieth century.

The most highly visible of these is cable television. Before the end of the 1980s, the number of viewers watching religious telecasts over cable television will probably exceed the number of people watching such programs on over-the-air television. This will be an especially significant development for small-town churches. In these communities, cable TV is opening the doors for hundreds of congregations to strengthen their community image and outreach through four to ten hours of telecasting every week. Will your congregation be one of these?

In larger cities, where the competition to be on cable will be far greater, church-owned, low-power stations will enable some congregations to reach neighborhood groups, including those who are not comfortable in the English language.

The second trend will be limited largely to perhaps a half dozen denominations during the 1980s. By 1990, a very large number of United Methodist, Presbyterian, Lutheran,

What Will Tomorrow Bring?

United Church of Christ, and United Church of Canada small-membership churches will be served by women pastors. In these denominations, the small church has been the traditional entry point (along with the position of associate minister in larger congregations) for people graduating from seminary. Women have not been an exception to that generalization. By 1990, as many as one fourth to one third of the small-membership churches in these denominations may be served by women ministers.

The most speculative of these projections is based on the assumption there is a long-term, cyclical nature to the American culture. There is considerable evidence accumulating that, by the late 1980s, the impact of the sharp increase of the price of energy will have been absorbed by the economy, inflation will have abated, the babies of the post World War II era will have become mature and productive members of the labor force, foreign relations will have entered a new era of stability, and the world-wide rate of increase in population will have declined significantly. [1] This school of thought suggests the 1990s may become the "Golden Nineties" and offer a very supportive context for many institutions, including the small churches. In brief, hang in there! Things will be better!

The fourth trend already is clearly apparent and may peak some time during the last half of the 1980s. This is the new religious revival in general, and in particular the "return to the churches" of millions of young parents born during the post-1945 era. During the late 1970s, new records were set year after year for the number of people attending predominantly white Protestant churches on the average weekend. In 1979, for example, the number of people present for worship in white Protestant churches on the average weekend was the largest in American history. (This generalization does *not* apply to Canada!) The big surge in attendance came in churches that (a) had been in existence for less than twenty-five years, and/or (b) averaged more than 300 at worship, and/or (c) were not related to one of the dozen largest Protestant denominational families, and/or (d) were located west of Pennsylvania and south of Interstate Highway 80, and/or (e) were at the conservative end of the theological spectrum.[2]

If this trend continues into the 1980s, what will be the impact on small churches located in the North and Northeast and related to the larger Protestant denominational families? The answer to that question may be influenced more by the openness, creativity, evangelistic outreach, and attitudes of the members, than by the local community context.

An overlapping trend can be illustrated by two pieces of trivia. In 1931, only 17 percent of all American physicians were specialists. Today, that figure is approximately 75 percent.

Second, as recently as 1950, a retailer could stock five different brands of cigarettes and satisfy 88 percent of the customers. By 1980 a retailer had to stock 58 varieties in order to satisfy 88 percent of the customers. Similar changes can be seen in the increased range of consumer goods and services, whether one looks at home radios, a high school catalog of academic courses, the program at the YMCA, or the shelves of the local supermarket.

These two examples illustrate two choices open to the churches. One choice is to be a small congregation with a clearly and precisely defined specialty in ministry. The alternative is to offer a broad range of programs and ministries—and that requires a large membership as the institutional base for the array of services. While it is an oversimplification to state that the choice is either to grow or to specialize, those are the two most attractive choices open to thousands of small congregations.

A sixth trend has been referred to earlier. This is the

urban-to-rural migration. For thousands of small-membership congregations in what once were rural communities, this reversal of the traditional migration pattern is bringing with it new and exciting, and, at times, frustration-producing, challenges.

The most profound change that will affect churches of all ages and types is what Daniel Yankelovich has described as the "search for self-fulfillment in a world turned upside down."[3] The willingness to give of oneself for others, to sacrifice for a cause, or to place the loyalty to an institution above one's own needs gradually has been eroded in recent years. This means (among many other consequences) that the churches have to use new approaches to enlisting and motivating volunteers, to financing mission efforts, and to creating new ministries in response to people's needs.

If one looks only at the subject of church growth, this emerging trend helps to explain the sharp increase in the number of church shoppers, the tremendous increase in the Roman Catholic–to–Protestant church migration of younger adults, the continued expansion of the Charismatic Renewal Movement, the remarkable increase in the sale of religious books while nearly all other categories of books have plateaued, the unexpectedly large response to direct-mail evangelism, and the tremendous increase in the number of people involved in Bible study groups.

If Yankelovich is correct in his diagnostic comments, this means a radical change in the rules in many different aspects of church administration and congregational life.

Finally, the next fifteen years will find thousands of small congregations accomplishing what they always knew they could not do. Some will open a Christian day school. Others will remodel their buildings to accommodate the physically handicapped. Thousands will relocate and construct new meetinghouses in order to accommodate newcomers from urban areas. Some will find that bivocational pastors are acceptable replacements for the full-time resident ministers they have been accustomed to for decades. Thousands more will conclude that women can be excellent pastors. Several hundred small-membership churches will be surprised to discover how many people accept the Saturday evening or Thursday evening worship service as a legitimate alternative to Sunday morning.

As the members respond to these changes, their faith in a living God as a creative force in the world will be reinforced.

NOTES

Chapter I

1. While many small churches do pay much more per member for ministerial support than does the typical large congregation, a variety of studies indicate that the per-member giving level of churches, both for total giving and for benevolences, is *directly* related to size. For the pioneer study on this, see the survey of over 5,200 congregations from fifteen denominations; *Church Size in Illinois* (Bureau of Research of the Church Federation of Greater Chicago, n.d.). For a denominational study, see *Comparative Statistics 1978* (Research Division of the Support Agency of the United Presbyterian Church). For another study that produced the same findings, see the *North American Interchurch Study*, Douglas W. Johnson, Project Director (New York: National Council of the Churches of Christ in the U.S.A., 1971), table 135, p. 120.

2. For this distinction between "attraction" and "proclamation," see Donald A. McGavran and Winfield C. Arn, *Ten Steps for Church Growth* (New York: Harper & Row, 1977).

3. Donald K. Campbell, *Personnel Statistical Study of the Presbyterian Church in the United States* (Atlanta: Office of Professional Development of the PCUS, 1980), part IV, p. 1.

4. Research on the dynamics of face-to-face groups overwhelmingly supports the concept that the point of diminishing returns is passed when the group exceeds seven people. For a summary of this research, see A. Paul Hare, *Handbook of Small Group Research*, 2nd ed. (New York: The Free Press, 1976).

5. Richard A. Gabriel and Paul L. Savage, *Crisis in Command* (New York: Hill & Wang, 1978).

6. For a more extended discussion of the centrality of these unifying principles, see Lyle E. Schaller, *Assimilating New Members* (Nashville: Abingdon, 1978), pp. 21-37.

7. Two very useful books that will help members of a small

congregation identify and affirm their strengths and resources are Paul O. Madsen, *The Small Church: Valid, Vital, Victorious* (Valley Forge, Pa.: Judson Press, 1975), and Carl S. Dudley, *Making the Small Church Effective* (Nashville: Abingdon, 1978). For an introduction to the planning model that is based on affirming strengths, assets, and resources, see Lyle E. Schaller, *Effective Church Planning* (Nashville: Abingdon, 1979), pp. 93-110.

8. Hart M. Nelson and Robert F. Everett, "Impact of Church Size on Clergy Role and Career," *Review of Religious Research*, vol. 18, no. 1 (Fall 1976), pp. 62-73.

Chapter II

1. J. William T. Youngs, Jr., *God's Messengers: Religious Leadership in Colonial New England* (Baltimore: Johns Hopkins University Press, 1976), p. 143.

2. The fundamental importance of widely supported goals is illustrated by the central emphasis given this point in current reevaluations of American high schools. See the essay on education by Fred M. Hechinger in *The New York Times* (April 14, 1981). Or see Iris V. Cully, *New Life for Your Sunday School* (New York: Hawthorne Books, 1976), p. 3, for a concise statement on why broad-based agreement on a specific goal is necessary for a strong church school.

3. A very useful study book on youth ministries for lay leaders in churches of all sizes is Glenn E. Ludwig, *Building an Effective Youth Ministry* (Nashville: Abingdon, 1979).

4. The best single source of data on attitudes toward giving is still the *North American Interchurch Study*, Douglas W. Johnson, Project Director (New York: National Council of the Churches of Christ in the U.S.A., 1971).

5. Ibid. pp. 111-26.

6. For a comprehensive historical, biblical, theological, socio-logical, and anthropological analysis of this point, see C. Peter Wagner, *Our Kind of People* (Atlanta: John Knox Press, 1979).

7. For an excellent guide to the value of advertising to church growth, see Steve Dunkin, *Church Advertising: A Practical Guide* (Nashville: Abingdon, 1982).

Chapter III

1. For an extensive analysis of the market for ministers, see Jackson W. Carroll and Robert L. Wilson, *Too Many Pastors?* (New York: Pilgrim Press, 1980).

2. For a more detailed statement of this point, see Lyle E. Schaller, *Understanding Tomorrow* (Nashville: Abingdon, 1976), pp. 101-5.

3. Dudley, *Making the Small Church Effective,* pp. 71-74.

4. Alvin Toffler, *Future Shock* (New York: Random House, 1970), pp. 325-28.

5. For an introduction to this concept, see John Y. Elliott, *Our Pastor Has an Outside Job* (Valley Forge, Pa.: Judson Press, 1980); or Doran McCarty, "The Bivocational Minister and His Ministry" *Associational Administration Bulletin* (Atlanta: Home Mission Board, March-April 1979), vol. 12, no. 2.

6. The best introduction to the larger parish concept, and an impressive apologetic for it, can be found in Marvin Judy, *The Cooperative Parish in Nonmetropolitan Areas* (Nashville: Abingdon Press, 1967). A useful newsletter on this subject *(Hinton Herald)* and on other issues of concern to small-membership churches is published by the Hinton Rural Life Center, P.O. Box 27, Hayesville, N.C. 28904.

7. For a very revealing case study that identifies the advantages and also some of the unanticipated consequences of a cooperative ministry, see Douglas Alan Walrath, *Leading Churches Through Change* (Nashville: Abingdon, 1979), chapter 4.

Chapter IV

1. For an impressive research study describing the impact of the teacher on the pupils, see Egil Peterson *et al.*, "A New Perspective on the Effects of First-Grade Teachers on Children's Subsequent Adult Status," *Harvard Educational Review,* vol. 48, no. 1 (February 1978), pp. 1-31.

2. Cully, *New Life for Your Sunday School.*

3. Andrew M. Greeley and Peter H. Rossi, *The Education of Catholic Americans* (Garden City, N.Y.: Anchor Books, 1968), pp.

85-92; 95-111. (It also helps for a child who was reared in a home with church-going parents to marry a church-going spouse.)

4. For several excellent insights on adult classes, see Dick Murray, *Strengthening the Adult Sunday School Class* (Nashville: Abingdon, 1981).

5. Benson R. Snyder, *The Hidden Curriculum* (New York: Alfred A. Knopf, 1971), pp. xiii and 12.

Chapter V

1. *The Milwaukee Journal* (November 25, 1980).

2. Waldo W. Burchard, "A Comparison of Urban and Rural Churches," *Rural Sociology* (September 1963), pp. 271-78.

3. Lyle E. Schaller and William E. Maloney, *The Church in Akron* (Cleveland: Regional Church Planning Office, 1963); idem. *Planning for Protestantism in Northern Summit County* (1964); idem. *Planning for Protestantism in Southern Summit County* (1964).

4. More recent church/population ratios can be derived from the county-by-county statistics on churches and church membership in Douglas W. Johnson, Paul R. Picard, and Bernard Quinn, *Churches and Church Membership in the United States* (Washington: Glenmary Research Center, 1974). It should be noted, however, that the figures include churches from only fifty-three denominations and thus severely undercount the actual number of congregations.

5. Theodore Caplow, Howard M. Bahr, and Bruce A. Chadwick, "Piety in Middletown," *Society*, vol. XVIII, no. 2 (January/February 1981), p. 34.

6. Edward W. Hassinger and John S. Holik, "Changes in the Number of Rural Churches in Missouri, 1952-1967," *Rural Sociology* (September 1970), pp. 354-66.

7. For a series of critical essays on the school consolidation social experiment, see *Education in Rural America*, Jonathan P. Sheer, ed. (Boulder, Colorado: Westview Press, 1977). For some significant "second thoughts" on centralized policy-making in public education by one who was the pioneering advocate of equalized financing for schools, see Arthur E. Wise, *Legislated Learning: The Bureaucratization of the American Classrooms* (Berkeley: University of California Press, 1979).

8. For an application of this concept to the rural church, see Edward W. Hassinger, *et al.*, *A Comparison of Rural Churches and Ministers in Missouri Over a 15 Year Period* (Columbia, Mo.: University of Missouri at Columbia, College of Agriculture, November 1973), Research Bulletin 999, pp. 21-24.

9. Arthur J. Vidich and Joseph Bensman, *Small Town in Mass Society*, rev. ed. (Princeton: Princeton University Press, 1968), pp. 231-41. For a humorous, but very realistic, description of this socializing process in the small-town church, see Peter J. Surrey, *The Small Town Church* (Nashville: Abingdon, 1981).

10. For an excellent statement on the centrality of preaching and worship in the small church, see William H. Willimon and Robert L. Wilson, *Preaching and Worship in the Small Church* (Nashville: Abingdon, 1980).

11. For a discussion of why the enabler role is the most difficult and demanding leadership role for the pastor, see Lyle E. Schaller, *Effective Church Planning* (Nashville: Abingdon, 1979), pp. 161-70. For a critical appraisal of the role of the public school teacher as a facilitator, see Robert Benjamin, *Making School Work* (New York: Continuum, 1981). For a very persuasive statement relating church growth to "strong pastoral competence" and a more aggressive initiating role for the minister, see the *Membership Trends* report prepared for the 1976 General Assembly of the United Presbyterian Church in the U.S.A. See also C. Peter Wagner, *Your Church Can Grow* (Glendale, California: Regal Books, 1976), ch. 4.

12. For a remarkably sensitive statement on both the costs and the benefits of a merger, see Gilbert R. Rendle, Jr., "Death by Merger," *The Christian Ministry* (July 1977), pp. 30-32.

13. What is widely regarded as the best book ever written on small-town America includes some very significant insights on the small-town church. See Vidich and Bensman, *Small Town in Mass Society*.

Chapter VI

1. For two very interesting approaches to the possible consequences of the post World War II baby boom, see London Y. Jones, *Great Expectations* (New York: Coward, McCann &

Notes for Pages 183-185

Geoghegan, 1980); and Richard A. Easterlin, *Birth and Fortune* (New York: Basic Books, 1980). Easterlin's record as a forecaster has been remarkably accurate in the past.

2. An examination of the belief and behavior patterns of the one fourth of the American population age 14 and over who are identified as "highly religious," can be found in *The Connecticut Mutual Life Report on American Values in the '80s: The Impact of Belief* (Hartford, Conn.: Connecticut Mutual Life Insurance Company, 1981). The contents of this remarkable study suggests that the aging of the American population during the 1980s will result in an increase in the proportion of the population who are highly religious.

3. Daniel Yankelovich, *New Rules in American Life* (New York: Random House, 1981).